40

PHOTOSHOP
POWER EFFECTS

SCOTT HAMLIN
SCOTT BALAY

40 PHOTOSHOP POWER EFFECTS

© 2002 friends of ED

First Published 2002

Trademark Acknowledgments

Published by friends of ED
30-32 Lincoln Road, Olton, Birmingham. B27 6PA. UK.

Printed in USA

ISBN: 1-903450-56-X

CREDITS

Authors
Scott Balay
Scott Hamlin

Contributing Author
Adam Swallows

Development Editor
Luke Harvey

Technical Editors
Dan Squier
Julie Closs

Author Agent
Mel Jehs

Project Manager
Simon Brand

Graphic Editor
Katy Freer

Technical Reviewers
Corne van Dooren
Bill Perry
John Flanagan
Nyree Costello

Indexer
Fiona Murray

Proof Readers
Victoria Blackburn
Simon Brand

Cover Design
Katy Freer

Managing Editor
Chris Hindley

CONTENTS

SCOTT HAMLIN

Scott Hamlin is the director of Eyeland Studio (www.eyeland.com), a Web content design studio specializing in online game production and original content design (as well as site design). Eyeland Studio is the creator of SwiftLab (www.swiftlab.com) and produces several products sold on CD-ROM and over the Web. Eyewire.com – the worlds largest stock imagery company – carries many of these products, and past clients include Nokia, Proctor & Gamble, Sun Microsystems, MTV Europe, Nabisco, and Extensis Corporation.

Scott is the author of numerous books including Flash 5 Magic, Flash 4 Magic, and Effective Web Animation, Interface Design with Photoshop, and CorelDRAW Design Workshop. He has also written over one hundred articles for industry periodicals that include Computer Arts Magazine, InterActivity Magazine, Web Review, and Web Techniques Magazine.

SCOTT BALAY
Scott Balay, a Denver r
(www.swiftlab.com) and Eye
with Photoshop, Scott also
clients include Nokia, Proct
and contributed to nume
Computer Arts magazine. In
and using it to make music
contemplating the platypus

Introduction by Scott Hamlin

Back when this book was little more than a vague idea, I knew that its main purpose would be to show readers how to produce a range of useful effects. Now while that was a worthy goal in itself, it begged the question: what effects should it feature?

When it comes to getting the most out of Photoshop, inspiration and creativity are essential ingredients, so the effects we chose needed to demonstrate both in abundance. I hope you'll find our final selection as rewarding to recreate as they were to dream up in the first place!

Presenting original ideas in a clear, concise way was essential to accomplish two key objectives: to demonstrate innovative effects in Photoshop, and to teach you how to be more efficient with Photoshop.

The explosion of the Web into all corners of life has helped push Photoshop far beyond its traditional role in print design. What's more, clients don't just want innovative and fresh visual effects – they also want them immediately. More and more, designers are called upon to create visually compelling masterpieces from scratch in ever-dwindling timeframes. In a world where your work can be published to the masses in the time it takes you to pour a cup of coffee, time has never been more valuable.

Third party plug-in filters can often provide a quick fix, but their long-term usefulness usually proves quite limited. It rarely takes that long for a popular filter effect to start cropping up all over the place, whether appropriate or not. Once that happens, you've effectively lost the whole "fresh and innovative" cachet that prompted you to buy it in the first place. It doesn't take a designer's trained eye to pick out the abuse of many popular third party filters. We may only have a short time to make our effects, but we rarely want it to *look* like they were done in haste!

The truth is that the more familiar you become with Photoshop's in-built facilities, the less you need to fall back on third party filter effects. In fact they usually just automate effects that you could have created for yourself, and experienced users should have little need for them, especially since the inclusion of all of the Aldus Gallery Effects filters way back in version 4.

INTRODUCTION

Now we aren't just trying to teach you new and innovative effects here. Our second – and equally important – objective is to help you get into the habit of using shortcuts and other time-saving techniques when you're working in Photoshop. The examples in this book won't just show you how to create an interesting effect – they'll get you using a plethora of easy shortcuts that will help to cut down the time it takes you to achieve great results.

Adobe provides a small tri-fold reference card along with every copy of Photoshop, listing many of the built-in shortcuts. If you haven't already done so (or lost it along with the box), take a little time to read it over – in my opinion, it's worth several times its weight in gold!

While the Quick Reference Card is a fantastic resource, there's no substitute for sitting down and putting the shortcuts into practice – that's just what the techniques in this book will help you to do. With practice, they'll become second nature, and you'll be able to create impressive effects in even less time.

Ultimately this book sets out to help you, the Photoshop user, to become more creative. The techniques we show can be used as they are, or serve as starting points and inspiration for your own ideas. As you become a more efficient Photoshop user, you should find you have more time and inclination to explore and experiment.

Have fun!

Finding your way around Photoshop
The main parts of the Photoshop interface are shown below.

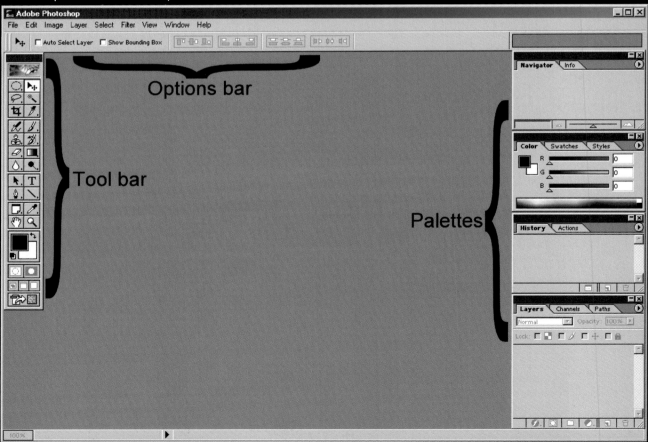

Each of the twenty-two buttons at the top of the Tool bar can be pressed to activate a different tool, and many give access to more than one tool – click and hold on them to find out what options are available. Below these, two boxes (shown containing the default colors black and white) indicate the current foreground and background colors.

The image at the left end of the Options bar indicates which tool is currently selected. The rest of the bar displays settings and options for that tool, which you can edit according to your needs.

The palettes contain specialized sets of controls and serve a variety of purposes, as you'll see in the course of the book. To access a palette, simply click on the appropriate tab, or click on the Window menu and select one of the 'Show' entries listed (e.g. Window > Show Channels).

It's worth noting that each palette features a small Options button ⬤ in the top left corner, which you can click on to access a host of useful options. In particular, the Swatches and Styles palettes both feature an option called Small List, which will show a named list of the entries in the palette – particularly useful if you need to tell your 'Light Red Orange' from your 'Light Yellow Orange' in a hurry!

A few tips before we begin

Default Tool Settings

All the instructions given in the examples are based on Photoshop's default tool settings, so you may find it useful to reset them all at the beginning of each example. You can do this by clicking on the tool icon at the left end of the options bar, and selecting Reset All Tools from the pop-up menu.

Naming

Renaming layers and channels isn't strictly necessary. However, you'll find it often proves very useful, especially when working with documents containing a lot of layers.

Keyboard shortcuts

We'll be making extensive use of keyboard shortcuts to save time and mouse-miles. If you find that one of these shortcuts doesn't do what you expect it to, it may be that you're actually tweaking one of the tool settings by accident. (In particular, look out for accidental changes to the Gradient tool's blend mode when you're using a SHIFT+ALT/OPT shortcut to adjust the blend mode for a layer.) If this happens, try selecting a relatively neutral tool (one without many settings of its own, such as the Move tool 🢂) and apply the shortcut again.

There's one very useful shortcut that we won't dwell on during the examples, just because it's so darned simple. If you're entering values in a dialog, you can move from one input field to the next by pressing the TAB button. SHIFT+TAB will do the same, but in the opposite direction.

PC users have yet another shortcut to fall back on. Each of the menu entries can be accessed from the keyboard, by tapping the ALT key, and then using the arrow keys to navigate. In fact, once you've pressed ALT, you'll see one character in each menu entry underlined (e.g. File, Edit, Image, and so on). Now you can just press the underlined letter on your keyboard to access that menu, and save even more time. So, pressing ALT, F, N will call up the New File dialog (the same effect as pressing CTRL+N). Likewise ALT, I, E, H will flip your image horizontally.

Guides

To position a new guide, click and drag the mouse out from either the horizontal or vertical ruler. Dragging from the horizontal ruler will create a horizontal guide, and dragging from the vertical ruler creates a vertical one. To reposition a guide, hold down CTRL/CMD, and then drag the guide to a new position. Guides can be removed by dragging them out of the image window.

Layer Styles

When you activate a layer effect from the Layer Style dialog, you should always click on the text of the button, rather than just checking the box beside it.

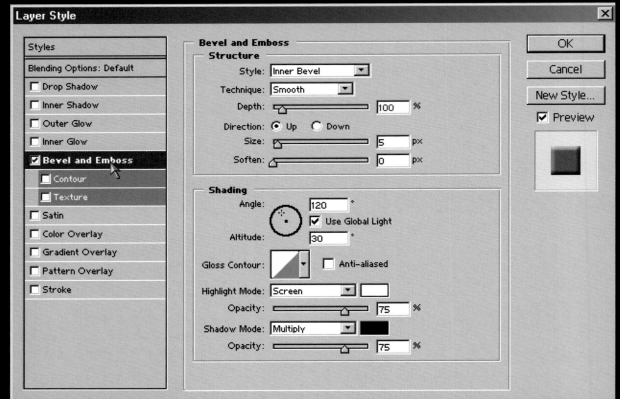

If you simply check the box, the options shown in the right-hand panel may not match the effect you're working on. You might think you're editing options for Drop Shadow when you are in fact editing the Bevel and Emboss options. Don't worry though – when you click on the button text, the check box will be checked automatically. If in doubt, take a look at the caption above the settings.

Resolution

All the examples are generated at 72 pixels/inch, with dimensions given in terms of pixels. If you want to use them in printed media (at 300 pixels/inch for example) then changing the resolution will simply make them appear a lot smaller.

In order to replicate the full-scale effects at higher resolution, you will need to increase the specified pixel dimensions accordingly. Say you want to produce a full-size image at 300dpi: when we say to create a 300px by 300px document, you will need to make yours 1250x1250 pixels (300 x 300/72 = 1250); if we say to apply a Gaussian Blur with a radius of 6 pixels, you will need to use a blur radius of 25 pixels (6 x 300/72 = 25).

As a rough rule of thumb, multiply all the specified pixel values by four to recreate the given techniques at print resolution.

Experiment

Don't forget: you should always try to experiment, and play around with the examples! The specific instructions given for an effect shouldn't be seen as the only "correct" way to accomplish it, but as one approach that happened to work for us. Your requirements (not to mention your taste) may well be quite different.

Files for Download

Some of the exercises shown make use of specific images (generally for background effects). In order to complete them precisely as shown in the text, you will need to download these source files from our web site www.friendsofed.com. Alternatively, you can use suitable images of your own. The download also contains PSD files containing the final result of each exercise, so that you can compare your results with ours more easily.

Support

If you have any questions about this book or about friends of ED, please check out our web site www.friendsofed.com where you'll find various contact details. Alternatively, you can mail feedback@friendsofed.com. We offer a fast, friendly and free support service: editors who worked on the book are available to solve any technical problems you may encounter.

There's a host of other features on the site – interviews with top designers, samples from our other books, and a message board where you can post your questions, discussions and answers, or just take a back seat and look at what other designers are talking about. If you have any comments or problems, please write to us – we'd love to hear from you.

SECTION 1: MATERIALS

1.1 Notched Metal

1.2 Woven Straw

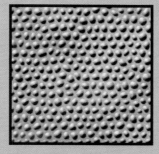

1.3 Quick Cobblestone

1.4 Basket Weave

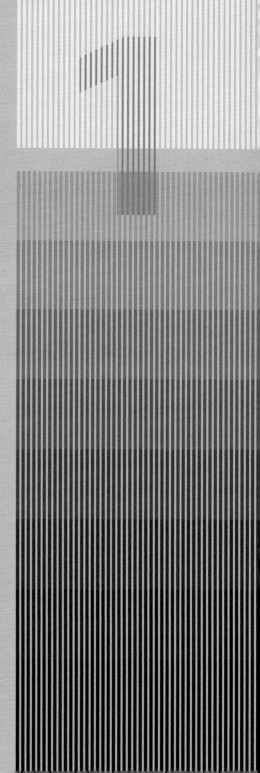

SECTION 1: MATERIALS

Notched Metal

We'll start off with a very simple method for simulating a textured metal surface.

1 Creating the 'metal' document

Press CTRL/CMD+N to create a new RGB document that is 20 pixels square at 72pixels/inch. Press SHIFT+CTRL/CMD+S to save it as metal.psd. Now press CTRL/CMD+'+' several times to zoom in to 1600%, and resize the window so that you can see the whole document.

Hit CTRL/CMD+R to show the Rulers. If the scale doesn't match the one shown below, press CTRL/CMD+K to call up the Preferences dialog, followed by CTRL/CMD+5 to select the Units and Rulers page. Set Rulers to pixels, and hit OK to continue.

Holding down SHIFT, click inside the left ruler and drag out a Guide (displayed as a vertical dotted line). Let go when it's in position halfway across the image (10 pixels) and it will change to a solid blue line. Do the same with the top ruler to position another Guide halfway down the image.

2 Defining colors

Open the Swatches palette and press M to select the Rectangular Marquee tool.

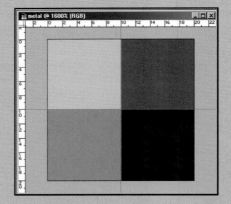

Click on 20% Gray, select the top left quarter of the image, and press SHIFT+ALT/OPT+BACKSPACE to fill it.

Repeat for each of the other quarters, using 40%, 60%, and 80% Gray for bottom left, top right, and bottom right corners respectively.

> You may find it easier to select specific colors from the Swatches palette. If you click on the button in the top right corner, and select Small List from the pop-out menu that this activates. The 'Small List' palette setting shows the color's name alongside each sample.

3 Defining the 'Notched Metal' pattern

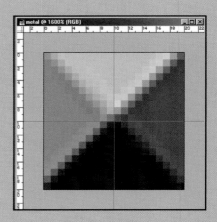

Press CTRL/CMD+A to select the whole image, and then select Edit > Transform > Rotate. In the Options bar, specify W: 150%, H: 150%, and △ 45°, and click on the ✓ button to apply the transformation.

Press CTRL/CMD+A to select the whole image again, and now select Edit > Define Pattern. In the Define Pattern dialog, specify the pattern name as "Notched Metal" and hit OK.

4 Creating and filling the 'metal notches' document

Now create a new document (CTRL/CMD+N) that is 400 pixels square, at 72 pixels/inch, and press SHIFT+CTRL/CMD+S to save it as metal notches.psd.

Select Edit > Fill and pick Pattern from topmost menu and set Custom Pattern to the new 'Notched Metal' pattern.

Hit OK to fill the new document with the pattern.

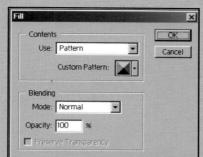

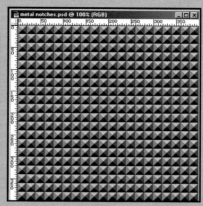

5 Adding variations in brightness

In the Layers palette, hold down ALT/OPT and click on the 🗅 button to create a new layer called "variations".

Press D to reset Foreground and Background colors to black and white respectively, and select Filter > Render > Clouds.

Now press SHIFT+ALT/OPT+O and then tap '6' to set the layer's blend mode to Overlay at 60% opacity.

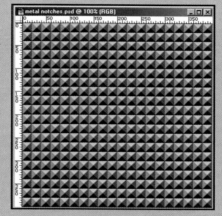

The clouds now subtly modify the brightness of the underlying pattern, and help the texture to look a little more realistic.

6 Adding some random noise

ALT/OPT-drag the 'variations' layer onto the 🗅 button to create a duplicate layer, which you should call "noise".

Press CTRL/CMD+BACKSPACE to fill this layer with white.

Select Filter > Noise > Add Noise, and set Amount to 100%, with Gaussian and Monochromatic settings both checked.

Now select Filter > Blur > Motion Blur with Angle set to -45 degrees and Distance to 100 pixels.

Finally press SHIFT+ALT/OPT+M and tap 5 to change the blending mode to Multiply with 50% opacity.

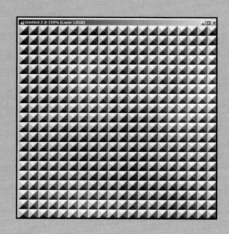

The Finished Product

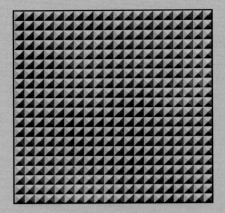

Notched Metal 2

We can create an interesting variation on the notched metal texture we've just seen by using a slightly different base pattern.

1 Creating the 'metal2' document

Press CTRL/CMD+N to create another new RGB document that is 20 pixels square at 72pixels/inch. Press SHIFT+CTRL/CMD+S to save it as metal2.psd. Press CTRL/CMD+'+' several times to zoom in to 1600%, and resize the window so that you can see the whole document.

Pick '50% Gray' from the Swatches palette, and press ALT/OPT+BACKSPACE to fill the image with this color.

Hold down ALT/OPT and drag the 'Background' layer onto the 🔲 button at the bottom of the Layers palette. This will create a duplicate layer, which you should call "notch".

Now select Edit > Transform > Rotate, specify W: 72%, H: 72%, ◣ 45° in the Options bar, and press ✓ to confirm. Hold down CTRL/CMD and click on the 'notch' layer to make the diamond-shaped selection shown opposite.

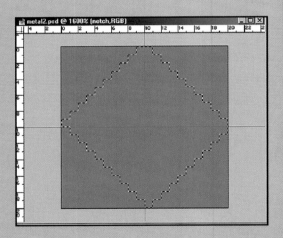

2 Defining the 'Notched Metal 2' pattern

Press SHIFT+CTRL/CMD+I to select the inverse of this area, and press G followed by SHIFT+G to select the Paint Bucket tool.

Pick '80% Gray' from the Swatches palette, and click in the top left corner of the image to fill this region with dark gray. Now use 60%, 40%, and 20% Grays to fill the other corners as shown opposite.

Press CTRL/CMD+A to select all, and use Edit > Define Pattern to create another new pattern, which you should call "Notched Metal 2".

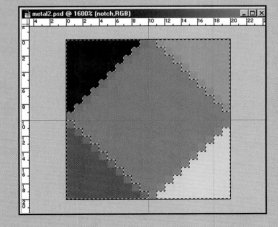

3 Creating and filling the 'metal notches 2' document

Open the `metal notches.psd` file from the first example (or from the file download) and press SHIFT+CTRL/CMD+S to save it as `metal notches 2.psd`.

Click on the 'Background' layer entry in the Layers palette to activate this layer. Now select Edit > Fill and pick Pattern from the Use menu. Choose the 'Notched Metal 2' pattern and hit OK to fill the layer.

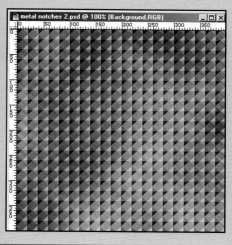

The Finished Product

SECTION 1: MATERIALS

Woven Straw

This method uses a similar approach to the Notched Metal technique, but adds a little color and random distortions to great effect.

1 Creating the 'weave' document

Press CTRL/CMD+N to create a new RGB document that is 20 pixels square at 72pixels/inch. Press SHIFT+CTRL/CMD+S to save it as weave.psd. Now press CTRL/CMD+'+' several times to zoom in to 1600%, and resize the window so that you can see the whole document. Hit CTRL/CMD+R to open Rulers, and drag out Guides to 10px across and 10px down, so that you can easily locate the center of the image.

2 Defining the 'Weave' pattern

Hit D to reset the default colors, and G (followed by SHIFT+G if the Paint Bucket is selected) to select the Gradient tool. In the Options bar at the top of the screen, make sure the 'Foreground to Background' gradient ▬▬▬ is selected, and press ◼ to specify a diamond-shaped gradient.

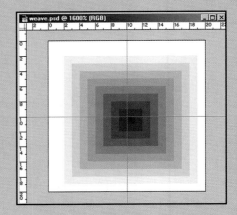

Now click on the center of the document, drag right up into the top left corner, and release to produce the gradient shown opposite.

Press CTRL/CMD+A to select the whole image and then use Edit > Define Pattern to define a pattern called "Weave".

3 Creating and filling the 'woven straw' document

Press CTRL/CMD+N to create a new RGB image that is 400 pixels high and 600 pixels wide, at 72 pixels/inch. Press SHIFT+CTRL/CMD+S to save it as woven straw.psd. You may wish to press CTRL/CMD+R and turn off the rulers at this point.

Select Edit > Fill and specify Use: Pattern with the 'Weave' pattern selected. Hit OK to fill the document with the pattern.

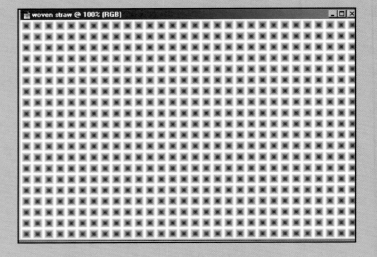

4 Distorting and colorizing the woven straw

Now select Filter > Distort > Ocean Ripple, set Ripple Size to 2, Ripple Magnitude to 7, and hit OK to apply.

Press CTRL/CMD+U to open the Hue/Saturation dialog. First check the Colorize option, and then set Hue to 40, Saturation to 70 and Lightness to +10. Again, hit OK to apply.

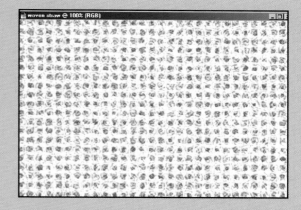

5 Adding dark highlights

Drag the 'Background' layer onto the ⬜ button to create a duplicate layer, and press SHIFT+CTRL/CMD+U to desaturate it.

Use Filter > Blur > Gaussian Blur with a Radius of 1, and then Filter > Stylize > Emboss with Angle set to 135°, Height to 1, and Amount to 150%. Hit OK to apply.

Finally, use the dropdown menu at the top of the Layers palette to change the blending mode to Hard Light.

Adding dark highlights to the texture makes it look more realistic.

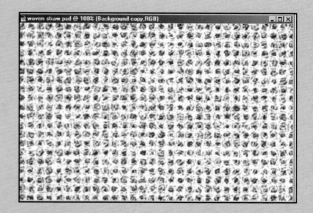

The Finished Product

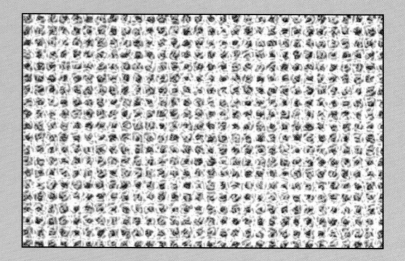

SECTION 1: MATERIALS

Quick Cobblestones

How about giving your projects a bit of a rustic feel by recreating the look of a cobblestone path?

1 Creating the 'cobblestones' document

First, ALT/OPT-click on 'Pale Cool Brown' in the Swatches palette to set the Background color.

Then press CTRL/CMD+N to create a new RGB document that is 400 pixels square at 72 pixels/inch, and be sure to specify Background Color for the Contents. Hit OK. Now press SHIFT+CTRL/CMD+S to save it as cobblestones.psd.

2 Creating the 'stones' channel

In the Channels palette, ALT/OPT-click on ⬛ to create a new channel called "stones".

Press D to select default colors, X to swap them round, and CTRL/CMD+BACKSPACE to fill the 'stones' channel with the current background color (white).

Now select Filter > Texture > Stained Glass. Set Cell Size to 10, Border Thickness to 6 and Light Intensity to 3, and hit OK to apply the texture.

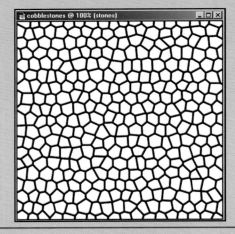

3 Rounding the stones

Apply Filter > Blur > Gaussian Blur with a radius of 3.0. Then press CTRL/CMD+L to open the Levels dialog, set the Input Levels to 150, 1.00, and 190 respectively, and hit OK to confirm.

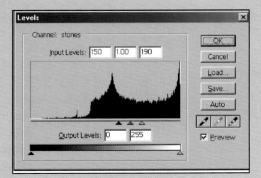

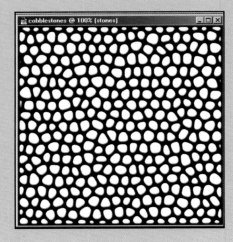

4 Coloring the cobbles

Load the 'stones' channel as a selection by CTRL/CMD-clicking on its entry in the Channels palette.

Switch to the Layers palette, and ALT/OPT-click on 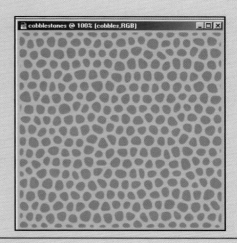 to create a new layer called "cobbles".

Click on 'Light Cool Brown' in the Swatches palette to select it as the foreground color, and select Edit > Fill to fill the current selection with this color. Press CTRL/CMD+D to drop the selection, and check the box next to ☐ in the Layers palette to preserve the transparency of the 'cobbles' layer.

5 Bevelling the cobblestones

Click on 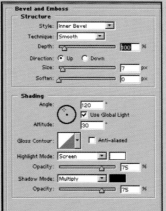 at the bottom of the Layers palette and select Bevel and Emboss from the pop-up menu.

In the Layer Style dialog, set the Depth to 150% and Size to 10 pixels. Leave the other settings at their default values and hit OK.

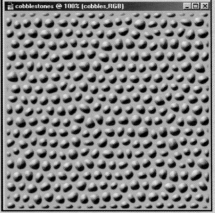

6 Adding a little noise

With the 'cobbles' layer still selected, select Filter > Noise > Add Noise, with Amount set to 5%, Distribution: Gaussian, and Monochromatic turned on. Select the 'Background' layer and press CTRL/CMD+F to apply the same filter again.

Click on  at the bottom of the Layers palette and this time select Drop Shadow from the pop-up menu. In the Layer Style dialog, set Opacity to 30%, Distance to 2px, and Size to 2px. Hit OK to confirm.

15

7 Varying the brightness

Hit D to reset the default colors and ALT/OPT-click on 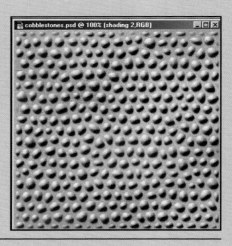 to create a new layer called "shading". Place this layer between the original two and select Filter > Render > Clouds. Press SHIFT+ALT/OPT+B, and tap '2' to change this layer's blend mode to Color Burn with 20% Opacity.

Finally, add one more layer called "shading 2" to the top of the stack, press CTRL/CMD+F to reapply the Clouds filter, and set the blend mode to Color Dodge (using the Layers palette or SHIFT+ ALT/OPT+D) with 25% opacity.

The Finished Product

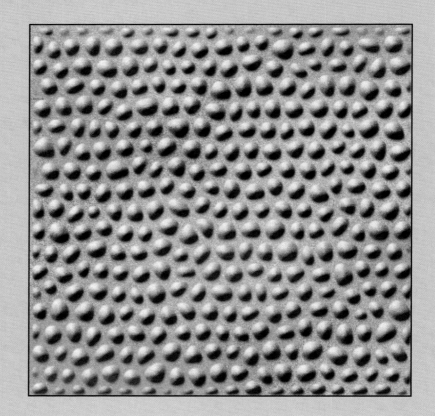

Basket Weave

One traditional surface texture that we can recreate in next to no time is that of a wicker basket.

1 Creating the 'weave' document

Press CTRL/CMD+N to create a new RGB image that is 50 pixels high and 50 pixels wide at 72pixels/inch, with a white background. Hit SHIFT+CTRL/CMD+S and save it as weave.psd.

Next, open the Navigator palette and drag the slider towards the right until the magnification is roughly 1000%. Drag out the corner of the image window until you can see the whole canvas, and if necessary, press CTRL/CMD+R to show Rulers.

2 Defining the 'basket weave' pattern

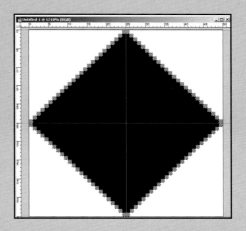

Drag three vertical guides from the side ruler and place them at 0, 25, and 50 pixels across. Now drag three horizontal guides from the top ruler and place them at 0, 25, and 50 pixels down. Press L followed by SHIFT+L to select the Polygonal Lasso tool, and use it to create a diamond-shaped selection.

Press D to set the default colors and ALT/OPT+BACKSPACE to fill this selection with the foreground color (black). Now press CTRL/CMD+A to select the whole canvas and select Edit > Define Pattern. Name the pattern "basket weave".

3 Creating and filling the 'basketweave' document

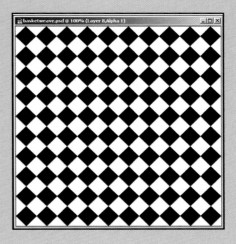

Now create a new RGB document that's 500 pixels high, 500 pixels wide, and 72 pixels/inch. Hit SHIFT+CTRL/CMD+S and save it as basketweave.psd.

Open the Channels palette and click on ⬛ to create a new channel, which will be automatically named as 'Alpha 1'. Use Edit > Fill to fill this channel with the 'basket weave' pattern, and CTRL/CMD-click on its palette entry to load the contents as a selection.

4 Graying the image out

First, open the Swatches palette and click on the appropriate entry to set the Foreground color to 50% Gray.

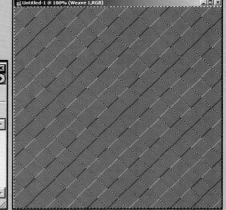

Now go to the Layers palette and ALT/OPT-click on 🔲 to create a new layer called "Weave 1". Press ALT/OPT+BACKSPACE to flood fill the selection with gray, and check the 🔲 box to lock transparency.

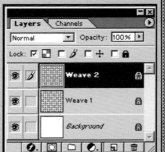

Now press SHIFT+CTRL/CMD+I to invert the selection, create another layer named "Weave 2" and press ALT/OPT+BACKSPACE again to flood fill the modified selection with gray. Once again, check the 🔲 box to lock the transparency.

5 Adding highlights

Press CTRL/CMD+D to drop the selection.

Activate the 'Weave 1' layer and apply Filter > Noise > Add Noise with Amount set to 30%, Distribution set to Gaussian, and the Monochromatic option turned on.

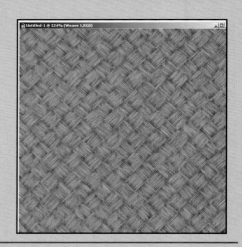

Next, activate the 'Weave 2' layer, and press CTRL/CMD+F to reapply the same filter. Then apply Filter > Blur > Motion Blur with Angle set to 45 degrees and Distance to 20 pixels.

Activate the 'Weave 1' layer again, and select Filter > Blur > Motion Blur. Change the Angle to -45 degrees and hit OK to apply the motion blur.

6 Embossing the weave

Hold down ALT/OPT and drag the 'Weave 1' layer onto the 🔲 button to create a duplicate called "Weave 1 Emboss". Do the same with layer 'Weave 2' to create a duplicate layer called "Weave 2 Emboss".

Apply the Filter > Blur > Blur More filter to both new layers, followed by the Filter > Stylize > Emboss filter (with Angle set to 90 degrees, Height set to 1, and Amount set to 300%). Change the blend mode for both layers to Hard Light.

7 Brightness variations pt.1

Back in the Channels palette, ALT/OPT-drag the 'Alpha 1' channel onto ⬛ to create a duplicate channel called "Weave 1 Blur".

Select Filter > Blur > Motion Blur and apply with Angle set to 45 degrees and Distance set to 40 pixels.

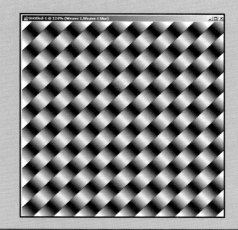

8 Brightness variations pt.2

Create another duplicate of the 'Alpha 1' channel called "Weave 2 Blur", and apply Filter > Blur > Motion Blur with Angle set to -45 degrees and Distance set to 40 pixels.

9 Applying the brightness variations pt.1

In the Layers palette, ALT/OPT-click twice on ⬛ to create new layers called "Weave 1 Shading" and "Weave 2 Shading". Press D to set the default colors.

Select the 'Weave 1 Shading' layer. Press CTRL/CMD+ALT/OPT+5 to load the 'Weave 1 Blur' channel as a selection, SHIFT+F7 to invert this selection, and ALT/OPT+BACKSPACE to fill it with black. Now press CTRL/CMD+ALT/OPT+4 to load the 'Alpha 1' channel as a selection, SHIFT+F7 to invert it, and DELETE to erase its contents.

SECTION 1: MATERIALS

10 Applying the brightness variations pt.2

Select "Weave 2 Shading". Press CTRL/CMD+ALT/OPT+6 to load the 'Weave 2 Blur' channel as a selection, SHIFT+F7 to invert this selection, and ALT/OPT+BACKSPACE to fill it with black. Now press CTRL/CMD+ALT/OPT+4 to load the 'Alpha 1' channel as a selection, SHIFT+F7 to invert it, and DELETE to erase its contents.

Press CTRL/CMD+D to drop the selection.

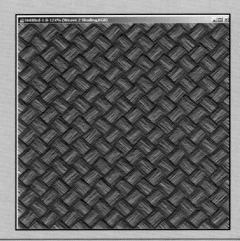

11 Colorizing the image

Select Layer > New Adjustment Layer > Hue/Saturation, turn on the Colorize option, and set Hue to 29, Saturation to 40, and Lightness to -5.

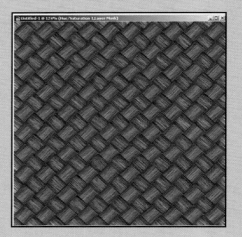

12 Saturation variations

Select Layer > New Adjustment Layer > Hue/Saturation. Change Saturation to 30 and Lightness to -45, and press OK to apply.

Now click on the layer mask and select Filter > Render > Clouds to apply the Clouds filter to the layer mask. Change the blend mode for this layer to Screen.

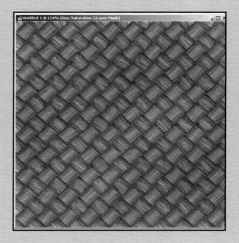

13 Darkening the dark bits

To increase the depth of the weaves, duplicate the 'Weave 1 Shading' and 'Weave 2 Shading' layers and set both their opacities to 50%.

Select the Layer > New Adjustment Layer > Levels. Set the second of the Input Levels to 0.23 and hit OK. Change the blend mode to Color Dodge with 50% opacity.

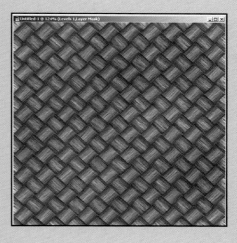

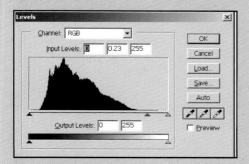

The Finished Product

SECTION 1: MATERIALS

Variations and Applications

SECTION 2: EARTH

2.1 Cracked Earth

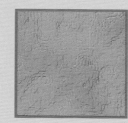

2.2 Clay

2.3 Stucco

2.4 Planet

Cracked Earth Texture

Let's say you want to add an earthy texture to your design – something that looks like a dry riverbed or the surface of Death Valley. You could drive into the hot desert and take some photos, but what if you want to save some time and do it without going out into the heat? Well listen up, because I'm about to show you how!

1 The 'color' layer

Press CTRL/CMD+N to create a new RGB image sized 512x512 pixels, with a white background, and save it as earth.psd.

Pick a good earthy base color from the Swatches palette, and press G followed by SHIFT+G to select the Paint Bucket tool. Click on the canvas to fill the image with this color.

> For ease of reference, you may want to view the Layers palette, double-click on the name of the default 'Background' layer and rename it 'color'.

2 The 'clouds' layer

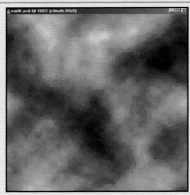

Hit SHIFT+CTRL/CMD+N to create a new layer called "clouds", followed by D to set foreground/background colors to black and white.

Select Filter > Render > Clouds to apply a Clouds filter, and then select Filter > Pixelate > Crystallize, use the default Cell Size of 10 and hit OK to crystallize your clouds layer.

> The Clouds filter provides us with a good starting texture to work with. The Crystallize filter then gives it a jumbled, blocky look.

3 The 'relief 1' layer

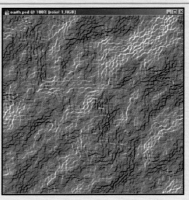

Duplicate the 'clouds' layer by dragging and dropping it onto the new layer button.

Hold down ALT/OPT and double-click on the 'clouds' layer entry in the Layers palette. When prompted, rename the copy "relief 1".

Select Filter > Stylize > Emboss to emboss this layer using the default settings Angle: 135, Amount: 100%, and setting Height to 2 pixels. Now hit OK.

Finally, hit SHIFT+CTRL/CMD+L to maximize the image contrast.

> The Emboss filter provides dimension by creating highlights and shadows along lines of contrast.

Note: The image dimensions we use here are very important, as we need an image whose dimensions (in pixels) are both multiples of 256. When this is the case, the Clouds filter (which we shall be using quite frequently) will automatically create a seamless tiling texture as its pattern repeats every 256 pixels. Seamless images can be tiled continuously such that you can't tell where the image's real boundaries are. Also bear in mind that the Clouds filter generates cloud effects at random – so don't worry if your results don't exactly match the ones shown.

4 Adding color

Press CTRL/CMD+U to open the Hue/Saturation dialog. Check the Colorize box, and adjust the sliders so that Hue is set to 20, Saturation to 40, and Lightness to -40 to get the nice red-brown hue below. Hit OK when you're done.

5 Blending layers pt.1

It's time to let these three layers interact with each other. Make sure the 'relief 1' layer is still selected in the Layers palette, and select the Overlay blend mode from the drop-down menu at the top left of the palette with an opacity of 50%.

6 Blending layers pt.2

Select the 'clouds' layer and pick Soft Light as the blend mode with 30% opacity.

Our three layers now begin to interact.

7 The 'relief 2' layer

With 'clouds' still active, hit Layer > Duplicate Layer and name the new layer "relief 2". Select Filter > Stylize > Glowing Edges and hit OK.

You may want to drag this layer to the top of the layer stack and set its blend mode back to Normal (with 100% opacity) so you can see what you're doing.

8 Embossing 'relief 2'

Hit SHIFT+CTRL/CMD+L to maximize the contrast on the 'relief 2' layer. Pick Filter > Stylize > Emboss, set a Height of 1 pixel, and hit OK.

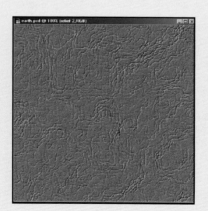

9 Blending layers pt.3

Set the blend mode of 'relief 2' to Hard Light, and bring the opacity down to 70%. Select Filter > Pixelate > Facet to roughen the lines a little.

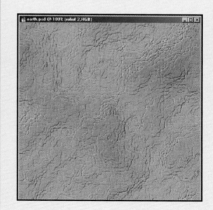

10 Adjustment Layer

Click the New Fill/Adjustment Layer button ⬛. on the Layers palette, and pick Gradient Map from the pop-up menu it reveals.

In the Gradient Map dialog, click the ⬛ button at the right-hand end of the gradient box. Press the ⊙ button next to the list of gradient presets, and pick Color Harmonies 2.grd from the pop-up menu that appears.

> *If you're asked whether you want to replace current gradients with "Color Harmonies 2", just click OK.*

11 Selecting a color gradient

Double-click the "Orange, Yellow" gradient, click on Reverse and then hit OK.

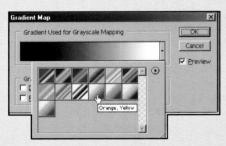
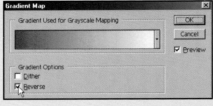

12 Blending layers pt.4

Select Filter > Render > Clouds and set the adjustment layer's blend mode to Color Burn, with 30% opacity.

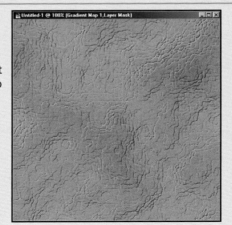

> *We are using this layer to saturate and enrich colors in the layers below it.*

The final cracked earth texture is made by combining 4 layers and a masked adjustment layer.

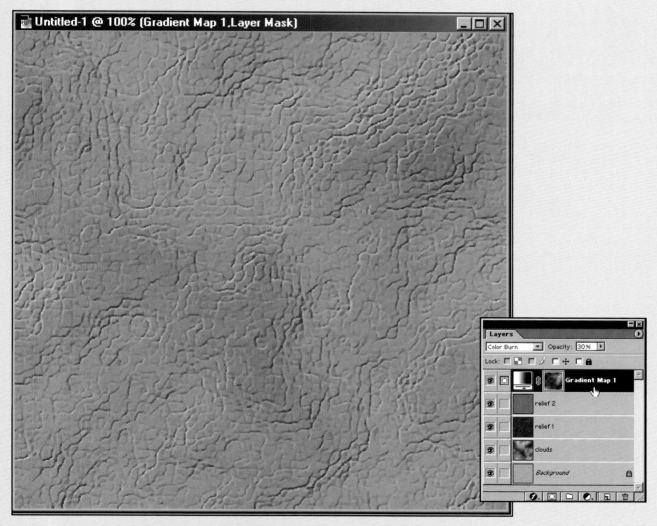

Save this file as `earth.psd` so that you can use it as a starting point for the other techniques we're going to look at in this chapter.

This texture – along with the others in this section – is seamless, and the techniques I've used here were developed specifically to produce that quality. You can quickly check how "seam-friendly" your image is by tiling it for yourself. Just press CTRL/CMD+A to select the canvas, and select Edit > Define Pattern *to define the selection contents as a pattern. Now create a new image, about 1000 pixels by 1000 pixels, and select* Edit > Fill, *specifying Pattern in the topmost field of the Fill dialog. You can now pick the earth pattern from the dropdown list just below, and hit* OK *to fill the entire canvas with repeated copies of the texture. Since it's seamless, you shouldn't be able to see where one tile ends and the next one begins – perfect!*

Clay Texture

Assuming you saved your cracked earth texture from the last technique, you'll be glad to know that altering it to look like clay is a quick and easy process. Open the earth.psd file, and save it as clay.psd, so that you have a separate file to play with and an unaltered copy of the cracked earth texture.

1 Adding color

Click on the 'color' layer to activate it, and press CTRL/CMD+U to open the Hue/Saturation dialog.

Adjust the Hue slider to your liking (I've opted for a rich purple-brown color: Hue:-100, Saturation:30, Lightness:-30)and hit OK to close the dialog.

2 Flattening relief 2

Next, activate the 'relief 2' layer, and choose Filter > Noise > Dust & Scratches. Select a radius of 2 pixels and hit OK.

This filter is principally designed for getting rid of small spots and blemishes. In this case though, it very effectively reduces the continuity of our grooved lines, making the relief look smoother, with flatter highlights.

3 Flattening relief 1

Activate the 'relief 1' layer, and hit CTRL/CMD+F to apply the Dust & Scratches filter once again.

After running a filter, Photoshop will place a link to it at the top of the Filter *menu for easy access. By selecting this shortcut (via the menu, or by pressing* CTRL/CMD+F*) you can quickly re-apply the filter with the same settings as used previously.*

You're done! You now have some clay to sculpt with. Like the cracked earth, this texture will not show any seams when tiled.

The layer palette: 4 regular layers and 1 adjustment layer.

The finished clay texture.

Stucco Texture

Like the clay texture technique, this technique is based on the `earth.psd` file we created earlier on. So before you do anything else, load up this file and re-save it as `stucco.psd`.

1 Applying Craquelure

Click on the 'relief 2' layer to activate it, and select Filter > Texture > Craquelure.

In the Craquelure dialog, you should set Crack Spacing to 8, Crack Depth to 2, and Crack Brightness to 9.

Hit OK. Bring down the opacity of the 'relief 2' layer to 50% to reduce contrast.

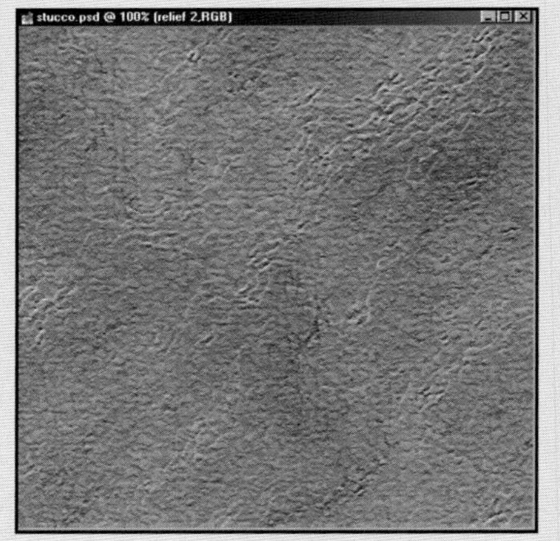

2 Softening relief 1

Activate the 'relief 1' layer, and choose Filter > Noise > Dust & Scratches. Set the radius to 2 pixels, and hit OK.

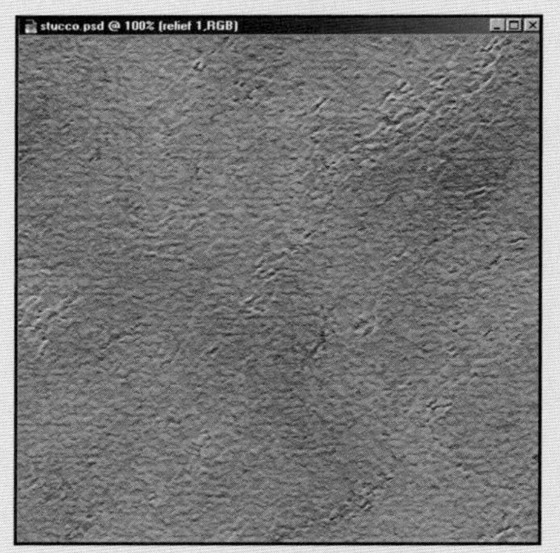

3 A new Adjustment Layer

Activate the Gradient Map adjustment layer, click on the Layers palette, and select Brightness/Contrast from the pop-up menu.

In the Brightness/Contrast dialog, increase both values until you get something that looks like this figure. Hit OK to dismiss the dialog. Finally, change the blend mode of the new adjustment layer to Screen.

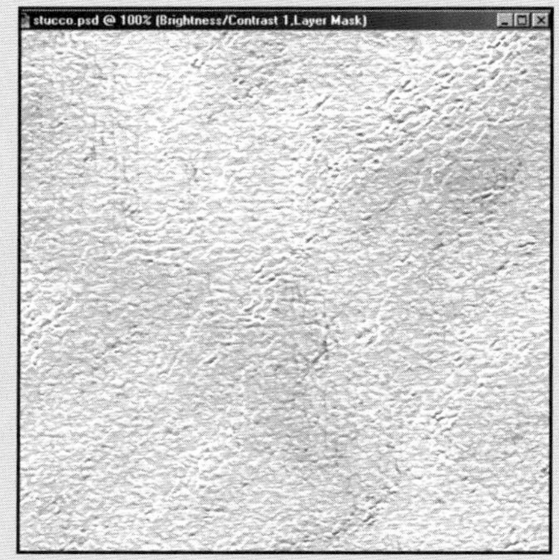

We increase brightness and contrast to give the appearance that a lot of light is reflected off the surface. I've used Brightness +50 and Contrast +25 to produce the image above. By using Screen *mode, the adjustment layer will brighten the texture, but reduce the unnatural-looking color saturation.*

Have you ever seen more a realistic digital stucco texture? It doesn't tile quite as seamlessly as our previous textures, but the edges are still fairly subtle.

The stucco's layer palette: 4 regular layers and 2 adjustment layers.

The finished stucco texture.

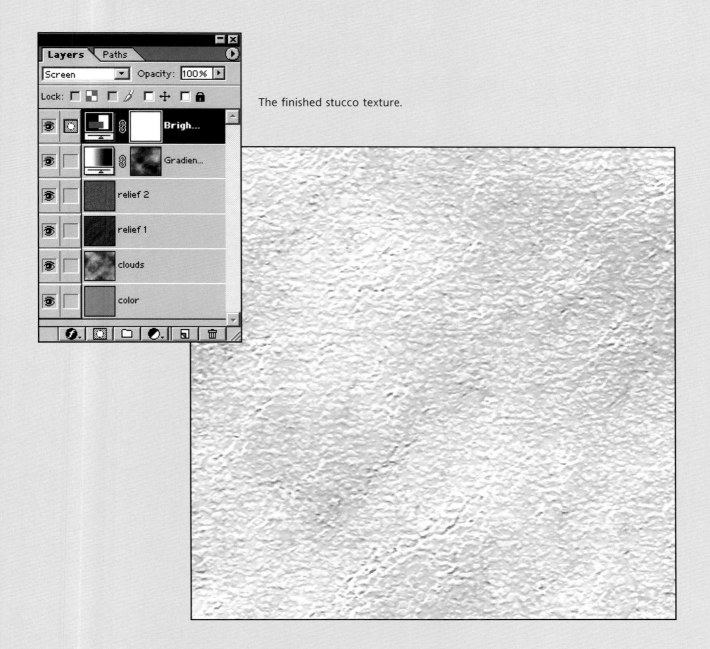

Planet Texture part 1 – the surface

In order to construct your own planet surface, you need several basic ingredients – continents, mountains, and oceans. Here's one of many ways to create a fictional, yet photo-realistic landscape of your own.

1 Creating the image

Hit CTRL/CMD+N to create a new Lab Color image sized 512x512 pixels.

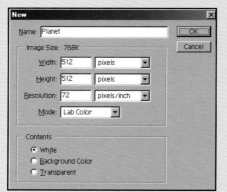

Call up the Channels palette, pick the 'Lightness' channel and select Edit > Fill. Fill this channel with 50% Gray.

2 Making clouds

Press D to ensure that the default black and white colors are set, and select the 'a' channel from the Channels palette.

Holding down the ALT/OPT key, choose Filter > Render > Clouds and Filter > Render > Difference Clouds. (Under Windows you'll need to hold down the mouse button as you navigate, or the menus will disappear.)

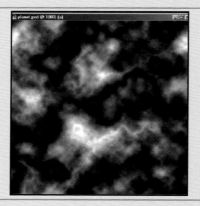

> The ALT/OPT key tells the filter to maximize contrast. If your image is displayed in glorious technicolor, it's probably because your Edit > Preferences > Display & Cursors > Color Channels in Color option is checked.

3 More clouds, more color

Repeat the last step, this time applying the Clouds and Difference Clouds filters to the 'b' channel.

Select the 'Lab' channel to see how the three channels interact to create color.

Select Image > Mode RGB Color to convert the image from Lab to RGB mode.

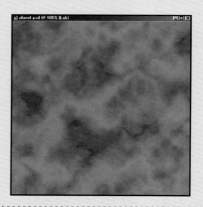

> The **Lab Color** mode is different from other color modes (like RGB or CMYK). In Lab mode, there are three channels that contribute to the image: Lightness, and two color channels named A and B. The A channel contains chromatic information from green to magenta, and the B channel handles blue through yellow. Lab Color mode is valuable when you want to adjust the contrast of an image without affecting color.

4 Gradient Map

Select the Layers palette, click on the New Fill/Adjustment Layer button , and choose Gradient Map. Open the list of gradient presets, click on the button ⊙, and select `Noise Samples.grd` from the pop-up menu that appears.

If asked whether you want to replace current gradients with "Noise Samples", click OK.

Double-click on the "Greens" gradient, and hit OK to dismiss the Gradient Map dialog. Now set the blend mode of the Gradient Map layer to Color, and bring the opacity down to 70%.

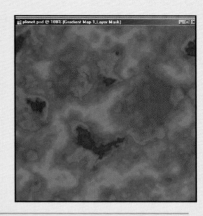

5 Colorization

Click the Layers palette  button and select Hue/Saturation. Check Colorize and adjust the sliders to produce a color suitable for continents.

I've selected a subtle green tone by setting Hue to 70, Saturation to 25, and Lightness to -10. Hit OK when you're finished.

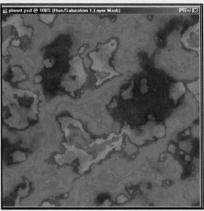

We use a Hue/Saturation adjustment layer to apply an even terrain color.

6 Lightening up

With the Hue/Saturation adjustment layer still selected, use Filter > Render > Clouds to add variation to the layer's mask.

Press CTRL/CMD+L to open the Levels dialog.

Change the value of the first Output Level from 0 to 90, and hit OK.

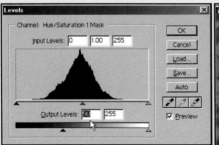

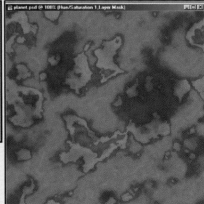

We push the brightness levels of the layer mask toward white in order to reduce hue variations.

7 Creating a merged copy

Press CTRL/CMD+A to select the entire canvas, SHIFT+CTRL/CMD+C to copy an image of the merged layers onto the clipboard, and CTRL/CMD+V to paste this merged image into a new layer.

The top layer now contains a merged copy of the other three layers. This new layer "Layer 1" will be used to define areas for the oceans.

8 Selecting dark regions

Choose Select > Color Range, specify Shadows in the pull-down menu labeled Select, and hit OK to confirm.

Now delete the layer containing our merged image ('Layer 1') by dragging it to the trash can button.

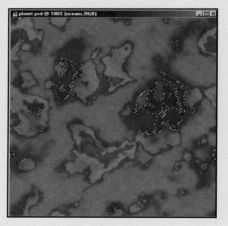

Here we are selecting the darkest regions of the image, and a marquee indicates the selected areas

9 Adjusting ocean levels

Open the Channels palette and click the ▣ button to save the selection as a new channel, and rename it "ocean map". Press CTRL/CMD+D to drop the selection.

Select the 'ocean map' channel and press CTRL/CMD+L to open the Levels dialog. Enter "9.99" in the middle text box and hit OK.

Double-click on the new channel and rename it "ocean map". Hit OK and CTRL/CMD+click the same channel to load it as a selection.

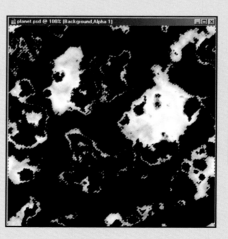

We set the middle 'input level' point to black in order to widen the oceans and add definition to the shorelines.

10 Painting the sea blue

On the Layers palette, click 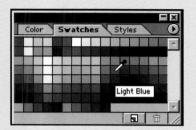 to create a new layer. Call it "oceans", and make sure it's top of the stack.

Use the Swatches palette to select a suitable color for the oceans.

Choose Edit > Fill, and select Foreground Color, 100% opacity. Hit OK and press CTRL/CMD+D to drop the selection.

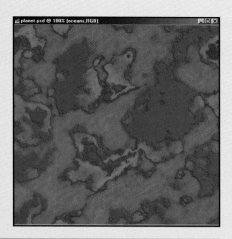

11 Adding beaches

Double-click on the 'oceans' layer, and select Blending Options. In the Layer Style dialog, click on Stroke and make the following adjustments to the settings: change Size to 1, Opacity to 20%, and Color to white. Hit OK.

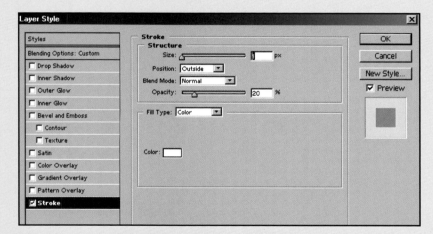

Finally, change the 'oceans' layer blend mode to Hard Light.

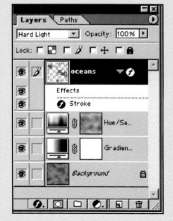

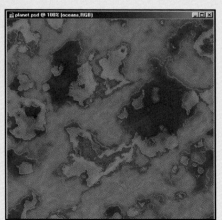

12 Adding Mountains

Call up the Channels palette and hold down ALT/OPT while you click the ▣ button. This will create a new channel, which you should call "mountains". Now make sure that this channel is active.

The merged image you copied to the clipboard in step 7 should still be available, so press CTRL/CMD+V to paste it into a new layer.

Press CTRL/CMD+D to drop the selection, and SHIFT+CTRL/CMD+L to maximize the contrast.

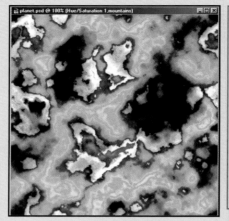

The mountains channel will be used as a "relief" map to give dimension to the terrain.

If you've changed the contents of your clipboard since step 7, you can get the required image back as follows: Hide the 'oceans' layer (by clicking on the ◉ button next to it), select one of the other layers, press CTRL/CMD+A and then SHIFT+CTRL/CMD+C. Don't forget to make the 'oceans' layer visible when you're done.

13 Lighting the mountains

Switch back to the Layers palette, and hold down ALT/OPT while you click the ▣ button. Name your new layer "relief", hit OK, and drag it to the top of the stack. Select Edit > Fill, specify 50% Gray with 100% opacity, and hit OK. Next, select Filter > Render > Lighting Effects.

In the Lighting Effects window, change Light Type from "Spotlight" to "Directional" and select "mountains" from the Texture Channel pop-up menu. Turn off 'White is high', and drag the circle and square symbols (representing light source and target respectively) until you get results resembling this figure. Hit OK when you're finished.

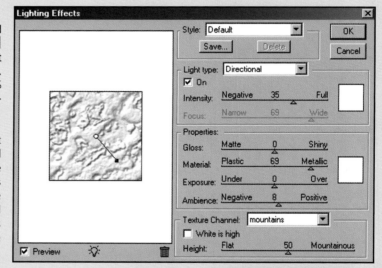

Select the relief layer, and specify Soft Light mode, with 40% opacity. CTRL/CMD-click on the 'ocean map' channel to load it as a selection, and press DELETE to remove terrain from the oceans. Hit CTRL/CMD+D to drop the selection.

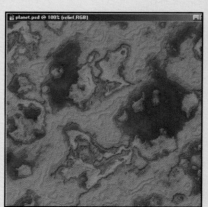

Planet Texture part 2 – the atmosphere

We could quite happily leave the planet texture at that; however, by adding a layer of clouds over the top, we can really give it an extra touch of realism.

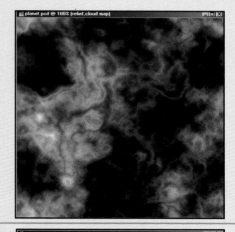

1 Complex cloud shapes

Press D to reset the foreground and background colors to black and white.

Select the Channels palette and ALT/OPT+click on 🔲 to create a new channel called "cloud map".

Activate the new channel, and select Filter > Render > Difference Clouds. Use CTRL/CMD+F to apply this filter 10 more times, adding complexity to the structure of the clouds.

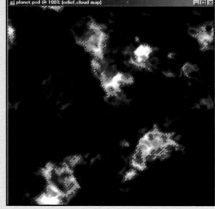

2 Thinning out the clouds

Press SHIFT+CTRL/CMD+L to maximize contrast, and open Filters > Noise > Dust & Scratches. Choose a radius of 2 pixels, and hit OK.

Press CTRL/CMD+L to open the Levels dialog. Set the central input level to 0.35, and hit OK to finalize changes.

Now CTRL/CMD+click on the 'cloud map' channel to make a selection based on its contents.

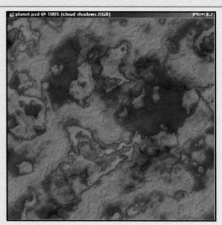

3 Casting shadows

Use the Layers palette to create a new layer (ALT/OPT+click on the 🔲 button), and call it "cloud shadows".

With this layer active, use Edit > Fill to fill the currently selected area with black.

Press CTRL/CMD+D to drop the selection and set the 'cloud shadows' layer opacity to 40%.

SECTION 2: EARTH

4 Little fluffy clouds

Activate the 'cloud shadows' layer and select Layer > Duplicate Layer. Name the duplicate layer "clouds", and make sure it's at the top of the layer stack.

Press CTRL/CMD+I to invert the clouds layer, making the clouds white. Bring the opacity up to 70%.

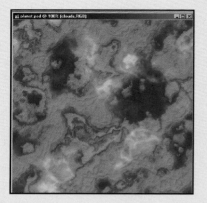

5 Offset clouds to create depth

Select Filters > Other > Offset and specify both horizontal and vertical displacements as −20 pixels. Be sure to set Undefined Areas to "Wrap Around", and hit OK.

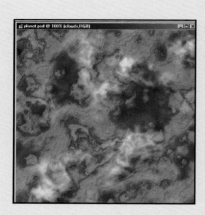

All done! It may have taken some work, but this realistic (although fictional) planetary landscape looks good enough to set up a colony on. For me, the most intriguing thing about this technique is that the Clouds filter is ultimately responsible for everything you see – color variations, cloud structures, even the shape of the mountains and oceans. Once again, the texture is seamless: try tiling it as a website background or as your desktop wallpaper.

The Layers palette: 5 regular layers (with 1 layer effect), and 2 adjustment layers.

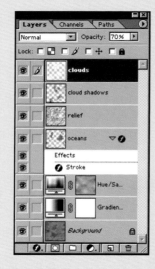

The finished planet texture.

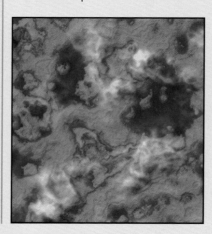

Variations and Applications

With the layers still available, you can make many changes to your texture without having to start over. I've created a few variations by editing adjustment layer parameters, blend modes, and colors.

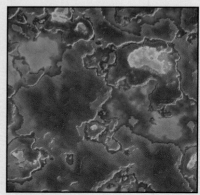

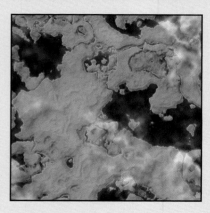

SECTION 3: WATER EFFECTS

3.1 Water Texture

3.2 Water Droplets

3.3 Pond Ripple

SECTION 3: WATER EFFECTS

Water Texture

Here's a quick technique that actually looks like water!

1 Creating a radial gradient

Hit CTRL/CMD+N to create an RGB image, making it roughly 500x500 pixels in size.

Hit D to set the colors to black and white, and X to swap them over (so the foreground color is white). Hit G (and then, if you find the Paint Bucket is highlighted, SHIFT+G) to select the Gradient tool [image].

Open the drop-down menu at the left end of the Options bar, and select the first gradient in the list: 'foreground to background'. Now press [image] to select Radial Gradient.

The radial gradient will be used to create waves centered on the upper left corner.

Click the cursor in the top left corner of the image, and drag it down to the bottom right corner. Release the mouse button to create the gradient..

2 Adding waves

Select Filter > Sketch > Chrome, and make sure the default levels are set (Detail = 4, Smoothness = 7). Hit OK.

Press CTRL/CMD+F to reapply the filter with the same settings, and repeat 4-5 more times until something resembling water appears.

3 Water color

Press CTRL/CMD+U to open the Hue/Saturation dialog. Check the Colorize box and adjust the sliders to achieve a suitable color for the water.

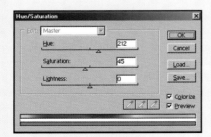

Then hit OK to close the dialog box.

4 Varying the brightness

Open the Layers palette, and drag the 'Background' layer onto the New Layer button 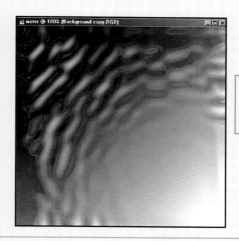 to duplicate the water texture.

Press CTRL/CMD+SHIFT+U to convert the layer to black-and-white, followed by CTRL/CMD+SHIFT+L to maximize its contrast.

Finally, select Edit > Transform > Rotate 180 Degrees.

This will be used to add brightness variations to the blue water layer.

5 Varying the color

Select Filter > Noise > Dust & Scratches, specify a radius of 20 pixels, and hit OK.

Change the blend mode of this layer to Difference, and bring its Opacity down to 30%.

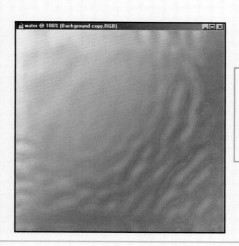

By using the Difference blend mode, we introduce some subtle variations of brightness and color into the image.

6 Changing the hue

Click the ⚫ button on the Layers palette, and select Hue/Saturation from the pop-up window to create a new adjustment layer.

In the Hue/Saturation dialog, turn on Colorize and adjust the Hue slider to produce a color that is slightly off from the water itself – 185 should do fine.

Hit OK to close the window.

In this case, I chose a blue hue that has a touch of green. This will allow for some interesting color blending.

SECTION 3: WATER EFFECTS

7 Blending the tones

Hit G to select the Gradient tool again, and with the same white-to-black gradient selected, click the Reverse checkbox in the options bar, so the gradient runs from black-to-white.

Drag the cursor from top left to bottom right, just as in step 1.

The gradient is used to partially mask the Hue/Saturation layer, creating a subtle blending toward a greenish hue in the lower right corner.

8 Adding Reflections

Press CTRL/CMD+A to select the entire canvas, SHIFT+CTRL/CMD+C to copy the merged image onto the clipboard, and CTRL/CMD+D to drop the selection.

Hold down ALT and press CTRL/CMD+V to paste the merged image into a new layer called "reflections". Make sure this layer is at the top of the stack.

Use Filter > Artistic > Plastic Wrap with the values Highlight Strength: 5, Detail: 9, and Smoothness: 7. Hit OK to run the filter.

Press CTRL/CMD+SHIFT+L to run Auto Levels on the layer, and run Filter > Noise > Dust & Scratches with a radius of about 5 pixels. Hit OK to close the filter dialog.

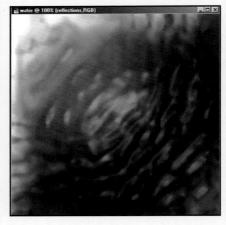

This layer will help to add reflections and make the waves appear to be flowing in all directions. The Dust & Scratches filter smoothes the waves out into simpler shapes.

9 Stirring it up

Finally, select Edit > Transform > Rotate 180 Degrees, and set the 'reflections' layer blend mode to Overlay with Opacity at 20%.

Come on in, the water's fine!

The waves now appear more chaotic and seem to emanate from the center of the image.

Finished Product

Variations and Applications

Shown below are a couple of examples of liquid textures that you can generate by simply changing the blend mode and opacity settings of the top layer.

Glowing Water (Color Dodge, 100%)

Thick Oil (Darken, 100%)

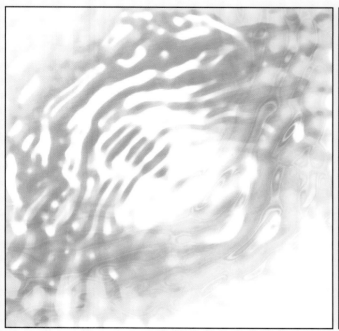

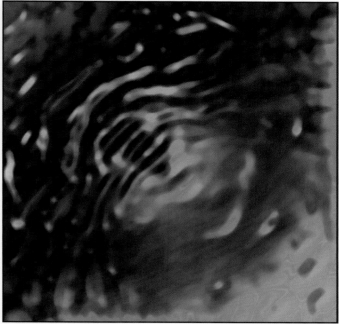

SECTION 3: WATER EFFECTS

Water Droplets

Adding splashes of water to an image is a nice way to add character to an otherwise typical picture. Depending on your choice of background image, the final result will either look like there's water on the surface of the image, or that the water's on the camera lens.

1 Background Image

Use File > Open to open up an image you'd like to cover with a splash of water.

I'm using a digital photo of a car I took in Glasgow. (I took the photo, not the car!) If you want to use it, open smart.psd *from the download folder. This car doesn't really need a wash, but it's getting wet anyway...*

2 Water Map (noise)

Open the Channels palette, hold down ALT/OPT, and click the ▣ button at the bottom of the palette. Name your new channel "water map".

Select Filter > Noise > Add Noise, set Distribution to Gaussian, crank up the Amount as high as it will go, and hit OK.

The Noise filter fills the canvas with random variations of brightness. It doesn't look like anything yet, but this noise will form the basis of our water droplet shapes.

3 Water Map (droplets 1)

Call up the Filter > Noise > Dust & Scratches dialog, set Radius to 20 pixels (with Threshold at 0), and hit OK.

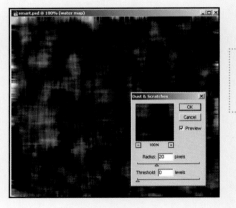

The Dust & Scratches filter helps to find coherent shapes in the noise.

4 Water Map (droplets 2)

Call up the Image > Adjust > Threshold dialog. Set the Threshold Level to 40, then hit OK.

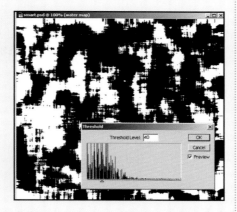

The Threshold feature converts a layer (or channel) to white and black. Pixels below the brightness threshold will be black, and pixels above will be white.

The white areas define where the drops will be, so this value ultimately governs the size of water droplets you'll get – a higher value gives you bigger drops, and a lower value gives you smaller drops.

5 Water Map (droplets 3)

Choose Filter > Blur > Gaussian Blur, set Radius to about 8 pixels, and hit OK.

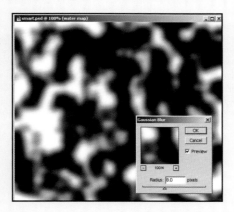

Gaussian Blur smoothes everything out, removing the jagged appearance of the shapes so that the white areas begin to resemble water droplets.

6 Water Map (droplets 4)

Once again, call up the Image > Adjust > Threshold dialog. Move the slider back and forth until you are satisfied with the size and shape of the water droplets and hit OK.

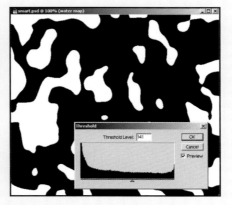

Use Threshold to get closer to the desired water droplet shapes.

7 Water Map (droplets 2)

Use Filter > Blur > Gaussian Blur once again, with a pixel radius of 2.

Press CTRL/CMD+L to bring up the Levels dialog. Just underneath the histogram in the Input Levels section, there are three triangles that you can drag to adjust the Input Levels. Move the black and white triangles towards each other until the droplet edges are well defined but not "jagged" in appearance. Hit OK.

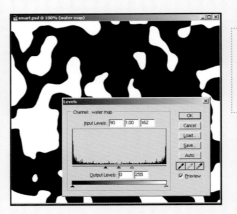

Using Levels with a blurred channel is a simple way to create smooth, well-defined edges.

8 Drops layer

Open up the Layers palette, hold down ALT/OPT, and click on the [ ] button to create a new layer called "drops".

Switch to the Channels palette and CTRL/CMD+click on the 'water map' channel.

Select Edit > Fill, specify 50% Gray and hit OK to perform the fill. Now press CTRL/CMD+D to drop the selection.

This creates the water droplet areas.

9 Drops (Bevel & Emboss)

Click the [ ] button at the bottom of the Layers palette, and select "Bevel and Emboss" to apply a layer style.

In the Layer Style dialog, apply the settings shown to the right:.

The bevel layer style makes the water droplets appear 3D — giving them depth.

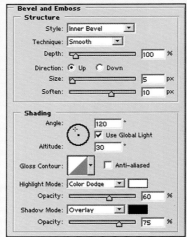

10 Drops (Drop Shadow)

With the Layer Style window still open, click on the Drop Shadow entry in the left pane of the window.

Bring the Opacity down to 30% and set the Distance to 3 pixels.

The drop shadow effect is subtle, but adds a degree of realism.

11 Drops (Stroke)

Click on Stroke, and set it for 1 pixel, 30% opacity, black. This gives the droplets a subtle definition around the edges.

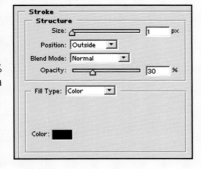

12 Drops (Gradient)

Click on Gradient Overlay, and select the "Black, White" gradient with an opacity of 20%. Check the Reverse box and hit OK to dismiss the Layer Style window.

The gradient helps to create contrast with the background. The top of our car image is very bright. By enabling Reverse, we make the gradient black at the top, flowing down to white at the bottom.

Because the top of the image is lighter, where the water droplets are darker, the difference in brightness makes the water more visible.

However, if you choose not to use a gradient overlay effect, the water will appear very clear and more transparent.

13 Drops (Soft Light)

In the Layers palette, select the Soft Light apply mode for the 'drops' layer.

The water droplets are starting to take on some realism.

14 Drops 2 Layer

Hold down ALT/OPT and click the [ ] button (at the bottom of the Layers palette) to create a new layer above the 'drops' layer – call it "drops 2".

In the Channels palette, CTRL/CMD+click on the 'water map' channel to load it as a selection, and use Edit > Fill to fill the area with 50% Gray, as we did in step 8. Hit OK to close the Fill dialog, and press Ctrl/Cmd+D to drop the selection.

Now set the 'drops 2' layer to use Soft Light mode.

15 Drops 2 (Bevel & Emboss)

Click the [ ] button to add a layer style, and choose "Bevel and Emboss" from the pop-up menu.

In the Layer Style window, set Direction to Down, Soften to 10 pixels, Altitude to 50 degrees, and Shadow Opacity to 0%. Hit OK to confirm.

This bevel effect will give the water droplets a second highlight in the lower right.

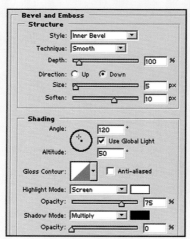

16 Distortion map

Click on the 'water map' channel to make it active. Press CTRL/CMD+A to select the whole image, CTRL/CMD+C to copy the channel to the clipboard, and CTRL/CMD+D to drop the selection.

Hit CTRL/CMD+N to create a new image, OK the default settings, and CTRL/CMD+V to paste the 'water map' channel onto a new layer in that image.

Use Filter > Blur > Gaussian Blur to blur the layer by about 5 pixels. Hit OK to confirm, and save this image as `distortmap.psd`.

Now close the window – we will be using the saved file later.

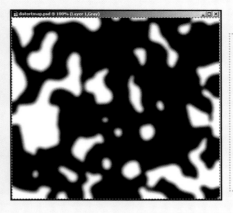

Save the blurred channel as "distortmap.psd".

Photoshop should automatically use the dimensions of the image on the clipboard for the new image.

17 Glass Distort

Return to the original water droplets document. Hold down ALT/OPT and drag the Background entry in the layer palette onto the ▣ button. Call the duplicated layer "distortion".

With this layer active, CTRL/CMD+click on the 'water map' channel to load it as a selection.

Select Filter > Distort > Glass, setting Distortion to 5 and Smoothness to 15. Select Load Texture… from the pop-up menu.

Navigate to the `distortmap.psd` file that was saved in step 16 and click Open. Hit OK on the Glass dialog to complete the distortion.

Note that the areas inside the selection have now been distorted.

18 Distortion lock

Press CTRL/CMD+SHIFT+I to invert the selection, and then press the DELETE/BACKSPACE key to clear everything but the droplets on this layer. Press CTRL/CMD+D to drop the selection.

At the top of the Layers palette, check the leftmost Lock box ▣.

This locks the transparency of pixels in the 'distortion' layer, allowing us to run operations on that layer without affecting the shape of the droplets.

A Distortion setting of 5 works well when using the Glass filter to distort photographs, but for line art, such as text or a logo, it might be too much. Try a smaller value, such as 2 or 3 for those kinds of images.

19 Distortion (Blur)

Run Filter > Blur > Gaussian Blur with a radius of 1 pixel, and hit OK.

Gaussian Blur reduces detail within the water's refractions.

20 Distortion (Contrast)

Run Filter > Sharpen > Unsharp Mask with the settings Amount: 100%, Radius: 1.0 pixels, Threshold: 0.

Unsharp Mask increases contrast in the refractions. You can skip this step if you prefer water with a slightly murky, out-of-focus appearance.

The Finished Product

That's all there is to it! Now you can splash liquid on top of any image!

Variations and Applications

It's very simple to change the color of the liquid. Hit the button at the bottom of the Layers palette, and select Color Overlay. In the Layer Style window, select a color for the liquid, set the Blend Mode to Multiply, and set the Opacity to 35%.

Swapping in a new background image can also be done very quickly without having to repeating the entire process. Just remove the 'Background' and 'distortion' layers, and replace them with another image you want to splash water on. Then repeat the steps starting with step 18.

Below are a few more of my own examples. For each one, I experimented with layer styles, apply modes, and color overlays and opacities to make the effect look as good as possible.

Pond Ripple

While we're considering water effects, let's investigate a unique way to create ripples in a puddle. The key to making convincing water is not so much in the ripple itself, but in choosing an appropriate image to reflect in the water. So, it would make sense to start with a view that looks up from a low height. A photo of some buildings taken from street level is a good choice – the sharp angle at which the camera is pointed will make the process easier.

1 Reflection Image

Open `building.psd`.

Now, if we were looking at this building through a reflection in a pool of water, the image would be inverted. Choose Image > Rotate Canvas > Flip Vertical. The building is now flipped.

2 Distortion mask

Create a new layer above the background, and rename it "ripple".

Select the elliptical marquee tool ⬭ from the toolbox. If it is not visible select the rectangular marquee tool ⬚ and then press SHIFT+M to toggle to the elliptical marquee. Draw a selection by dragging from the upper left toward the lower right.

While dragging, hold down SHIFT to constrain the selection to a perfect circle. The position and size are not important at this stage, but leave some empty space on all sides of the selection.

3 Black mask

Press CTRL/CMD+ ALT/OPT+D to feather the selection by 12 pixels, and hit OK to close the dialog.

Select Edit > Fill, specify Use: Black, and hit OK to fill the selection with black.

Press CTRL/CMD+D to drop the selection.

The feathered circle will contain different kinds of ripple effects.

4 Adding layer style

Click the "Add layer style" button on the Layers palette, and choose Inner Glow.

In the Layer Style window, change the Blend Mode to Difference, Color to white and Opacity to 100%. In the Quality section, open the Contour pop-up, and double-click "Ring – Double", the third style on the second row.

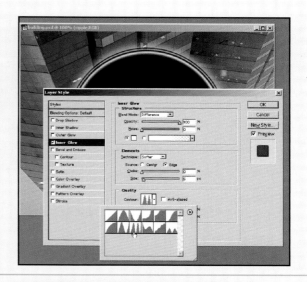

> The "Ring – Double" glow shape gives the appearance of three waves.

5 Sizing the ripples

Adjust the Size slider until the size of the white bands look appropriate for ripples in water.

Click OK when you've created bands similar to the ones opposite.

> You won't see anything that looks like an actual ripple in the water at this point; we're simply creating white bands that will eventually become waves. I set the Size slider to 140 pixels, but you may wish to use a different size, depending on the size of your circle shape.

6 Hiding a layer

This first ripple will be used to create more ripples of varying sizes. In order to do so, it is best to keep the 'ripple' layer as the source layer for each ripple. Start by clicking the eye icon to the left of the 'ripple' layer to hide it. This layer will remain hidden and will be used to create copies.

> The 'ripple' layer is now hidden from view.

53

7 Positioning the ripples

Drag the 'ripple' layer down to the New Layer button, which will create a copy of the layer, and make it visible again. Press CTRL/CMD+T to go into Free Transform mode. Drag the ripple to a new location, and move the corner points to resize it. When resizing, hold down the SHIFT key to keep a circular shape. Hit the ENTER key to finish the transformation.

Use Free Transform to create a ripple in a new part of the image.

Use Scale Effects to quickly adjust the ripple size.

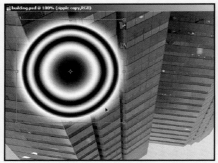

8 More Ripples

Repeat step 7 for each additional ripple you want in your scene. Ripples can be partially overlapped, and it is a good idea to place ripples that sit partly off the edges of the canvas.

I decided to use a total of 8 ripples.

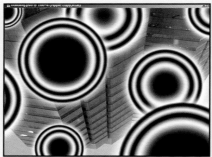

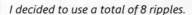

Each ripple is on its own layer. I closed the layer style views by clicking the triangle button on each layer to conserve space on the palette.

9 Tweaking the layers

On each visible ripple layer, click the box just to the left of the layer's name to link the ripples together. Then set each visible ripple layer to use the Lighten blend mode.

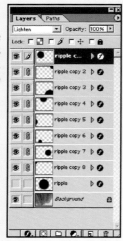

All ripples are now set to Lighten, and are linked together, as indicated by the "chain" icons.

The image looks a little strange now, but the Lighten mode in conjunction with the Difference mode of the Inner Glow lets the ripples interact with each other. Even though I scaled the ripple to a smaller size, the Inner Glow style is still being applied dynamically at a size of 140 pixels. If the resized ripple looks strange, you can easily adjust it through the Layer > Layer Style > Scale Effects dialog.

10 Adding perspective

Zoom out to 50%, or until you can see lots of "work space" surrounding the canvas. Then choose Edit > Transform > Perspective. Drag the top-left corner point to the right until the shape looks like the adjacent figure. Hit Enter twice to finish the warping.

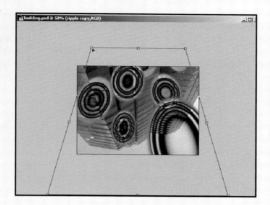

The Perspective transform tool makes an image appear to recede into the distance. The ripple layers are linked together, so the transformation applies to all of them.

11 Flattening the ripples

Press CTRL/CMD+T to enter Free Transform mode. Drag the corner points to flatten the ripples vertically until the shape of the ripples seems appropriate based on the perspective of the image being reflected.

Press the ENTER key twice to finish the transformation.

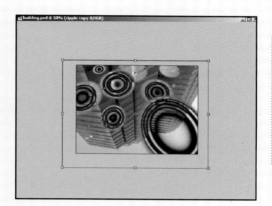

Flattening the ripples makes their perspective look more realistic. I don't have a scientific method for matching perspective, but a little experimentation can get you something that looks fairly real.

12 Fixing the ripples

Zoom in to 100%, or the original size you were using before the transformations. As you may notice at this point, some ripples may look a little odd. Transforming them will affect the Inner Glow layer style, as it did before. Use the Layers > Layer Style > Scale Effects dialog to make necessary fixes to the ripples.

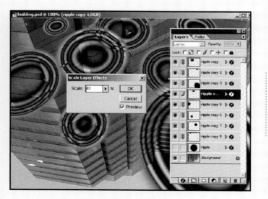

I used the Scale Effects dialog to make fixes to about half of the ripples.

55

13 Adding background

Create a new layer above the background image, but below the ripple layers. Set the foreground color to black, select all and then press ALT/OPT+BACKSPACE to fill the layer.

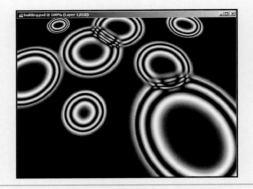

The black layer isolates the ripples from the background and allows them to blend with each other.

14 Saving the ripples

Choose File > Save As. In the Save As dialog, under Save Options, turn on "As a copy", and turn off Layers.

Save the file as `ripples.psd`.

This saves a copy of the ripples into a new PSD file. The specified Save Options will result in a PSD that just contains the black-and-white image of the ripples.

15 The Ripple channel

Press CTRL/CMD+A to select the whole canvas, and choose Edit > Copy Merged to copy the ripples to the clipboard.

Click the ⬛ button on the Channels palette, and name the new channel "ripple map".

Activate the new ripple map channel, and press CTRL/CMD+V to paste. Then press CTRL/CMD+D to drop the selection.

Paste the black-and-white ripple image into a new channel.

16 Duplicating the background

Go back to the Layers palette, and hide every layer except the background image. Hide layers by clicking on the eye icons to the left of the layer thumbnails.

Duplicate the background layer by dragging it to the New Layer button – name this new layer "distortion".

All layers have been hidden except the background image. A copy of the background has been made, which will be distorted by the ripples.

17 Distorting the image

Use Filter > Distort > Displace with the default settings of 10% Horizontal and Vertical Scale, Stretch to Fit, and Repeat Edge Pixels. Hit OK.

Browse to and open the ripples.psd file you saved in step 14.

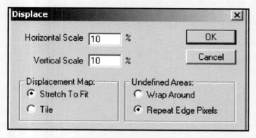

This filter takes a PSD file as input and uses it to distort an image based on the brightness values in the file. Notice how the ripples have distorted the reflected image of the building.

18 Adding shadow

Create a new layer above the distortion layer, and rename it "highlights".

CTRL/CMD+click on the ripple map channel to load it as a selection, and then choose Edit > Fill, select black, and hit OK.

Hit CTRL/CMD+D to drop the selection.

Set the 'highlights' layer's blend mode to Soft Light and its Opacity to 50%.

The Soft Light apply mode adds a subtle shadow to the ripples.

19 Adding bevel

Click the button on the Layers palette and pick Bevel and Emboss with settings as shown below. Hit OK to close the Layer Style dialog.

Now duplicate the 'distortion' layer as "distortion blur". Use Filter > Blur > Gaussian Blur to apply a blur of 5 pixels, and set the Opacity of the 'distortion blur' layer to 50%.

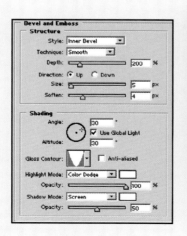

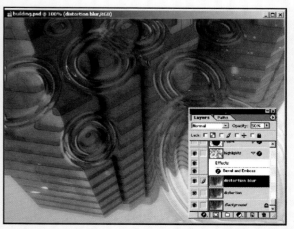

20 Ground Texture

Create a new layer called "ground", above the 'distortion blur' layer, open `ground.psd` and paste it into the new layer. If necessary, use Edit > Transform > Perspective to match perspective with the ripples.

Use Filter > Distort > Displace with `ripples.psd` to add distortions to the ground texture. Use small values (3%) for Horizontal and Vertical Scale, and keep the other settings as before

21 Blending in the reflection

Press D to set default colors. Set the ground layer's Opacity to 70% and press the ▣ button on the Layers palette to add an opacity mask to the ground texture.

Use Filter > Render > Clouds to add variation to the opacity of the ground.

Press CTRL/CMD+L and use the Levels dialog to adjust the distribution of light and dark areas in the layer mask until you find something suitable.

The Finished Product

Here's our finished example of pond ripples, with distortions applied to reflections and ground textures.

SECTION 4: SKY

4.1 Cloudy Text

4.2 Sunset

4.3 Nebulae

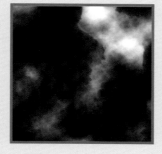

4.4 Starfields

SECTION 4: SKY

Cloudy Text

Tired of ordinary text with that flat, boring appearance? Add a unique dash of surrealism by turning your text into fluffy clouds!

1 The 'text' layer

Press CTRL/CMD+N to create a new RGB document, 667x500 pixels, with a white background. Press SHIFT+CTRL/CMD+S to save it as `cloudtext.psd`, and CTRL/CMD+I to invert the colors (so that you have a black background).

Open the Channels palette and ALT/OPT-click the ⬛ button to create a new channel called "text".

Press T to select the Type tool and use a sans-serif font such as Arial or Verdana to add the text "cloudy" to the center of the image. When you are happy with the shape and size of the text, click the ⬛ button in the Options bar, and press CTRL/CMD+D to drop the selection.

> *The text shown here is available in the download as* `cloudy.psd`.

2 Blur, Noise, and Distortion

With the 'text' channel active, go to Filter > Blur > Gaussian Blur. Set the Radius to 3 pixels, and hit OK.

Use Filter > Artistic > Film Grain with Grain set to 8, Highlight Area to 12, and Intensity to 4. Hit OK.

Open the Filter > Distort > Ocean Ripple filter. In the filter window, select a Ripple Size of 6 and a Ripple Magnitude of 6. Hit OK to execute the filter.

> *Blur the edges to soften up any sharp corners. Film Grain adds a lot of noise around the text border, while Ocean Ripple applies a heavy distortion to the edges.*

3 The fluffy effect

Select Image > Adjust > Threshold, set the Threshold Level to 235, and hit OK.

Bring up Filter > Blur > Gaussian Blur again, this time selecting a Radius of 2 pixels, and hit OK.

To finish off, use Filter > Artistic > Film Grain with Grain set to 0, Highlight Area set to 3, and Intensity set to 3. Click OK.

> *Threshold converts the image to black-and-white, bringing us closer to the fluffy-edged effect we want. Blurring removes the jagged edges and gives the text a softer look. Film Grain then thickens the edges of the text and adds definition.*

4 The 'clouds' layer

CTRL/CMD-click on the 'text' channel to load it as a selection.

Now switch to the Layers palette and ALT/OPT-click the 🔲 button to create a new layer named "clouds".

Press CTRL/CMD+BACKSPACE to fill the selection with white, and CTRL/CMD+D to drop the selection.

Select Image > Adjust > Brightness/Contrast, set Brightness to about -20 and click OK.

> *Bringing the cloud brightness down slightly will make it easier to add visible highlights.*

5 Adding a bevel

Change the 'clouds' layer's Opacity to 80%.

Now click the 🄵 button on the Layers palette and select Bevel and Emboss. In the Layer Style dialog, set Depth to 150%, Size to 20 pixels and Soften to 2 pixels. Set the Highlight and Shadow Opacities to 100% and 20% respectively, and select a dark blue Shadow color (R:50, G:50, B:100).

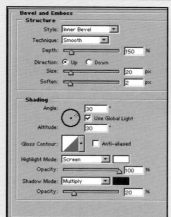

> *Using the Bevel/Emboss layer style adds dimension to the clouds.*

6 Contour and Texture

Still in the Layer Style dialog, click on the Contour button (just below Bevel and Emboss in the left-hand pane), click on the button next to the contour map image, and select 'Half Round' from the list of preset contours.

Now click on the Texture button to activate this layer effect and bring up its settings. Open the drop-down menu and select 'Clouds' from the list of preset patterns. Set Scale to 230% and Depth to 75%, and hit OK.

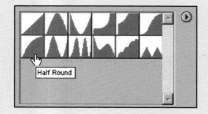

> *The Half Round contour gives a subtle enhancement to the clouds' bevel style.*

> *If you need to reset to the default patterns, click and choose Reset Patterns from the pop-up menu.*

> *The Clouds contour preset introduces variation into the consistency of the clouds.*

7 Adding a background

Open the file `spirals.psd` from the download folder, and press CTRL/CMD+A followed by CTRL/CMD+C to select all and copy it to the clipboard.

Now return to `cloudtext.psd` and press CTRL/CMD+V to paste in the spiral staircase image as a new layer. Drag it down the layer stack so that it's just below the 'clouds' layer.

8 Creating contrast

Click on the  button in the Layers palette, and select Stroke. In the Layer Style dialog, set Size to 1px, Opacity to 50%, and select a medium blue color.

Adding a stroke to the clouds adds contrast around the edges. Notice how they are now more visible, though still soft in appearance.

9 Adding shadow

With the Layer Style dialog still up enable Drop Shadow. Change the Blend Mode to Overlay, bring the Opacity down to 50%, and set Distance to 14 pixels. Hit OK.

The Drop Shadow effect adds that final touch of depth and allows the clouds to float above the background.

The Finished Product

SECTION 4: SKY

Sunset

Digital representations of sunsets can be almost as breathtaking as the real thing, and in Photoshop it's easy to create your own from scratch. I find these effects rather intriguing because they're based on randomly generated filter effects. So, just as you'll never see the same sunset twice, you'll never quite duplicate one of these Photoshop sunset effects.

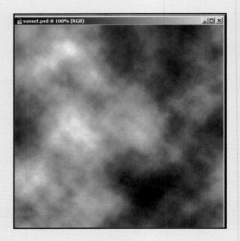

1 Creating clouds

Press CTRL/CMD+N to create a new RGB document, 500x500 pixels, with a white background. Hit OK. Press SHIFT+CTRL/CMD+S to save it as sunset.psd.

Press the D key to reset to the default colors, and ALT/OPT+BACKSPACE to fill the background layer with black.

Hold down the ALT/OPT key and click 🔲 on the Layers palette to create a new layer named "center clouds". With the new layer active, run Filter > Render > Clouds.

This fills the canvas with a random cloud pattern, which will be used as the basis for the clouds visible in the sunset.

2 Adding perspective

Select Edit >Transform > Perspective and a box will appear round the image, with control points at the sides and corners. In the Options bar set W to 30% and then drag the top left control back to the top left corner of the image. Press ENTER twice to apply the transformation.

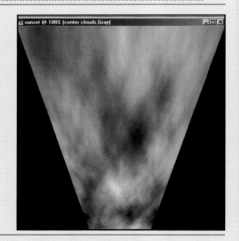

Distort the clouds toward a "horizon" at the bottom of the image.

3 Softening the cloud edges: feathering the selection

CTRL/CMD-click on the 'center clouds' layer to load its contents as a selection. Use Select > Modify > Contract with a value of 30 to exclude the edges of the clouds image from the selection.

Now press CTRL/CMD+ALT/OPT+D to call up the Feather dialog, and set Feather Radius to 20. Click OK to feather the selection, followed by SHIFT+CTRL/CMD+I to invert the area of the selection.

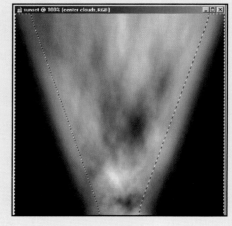

Use Filter > Blur > Gaussian Blur with a Radius of 20 pixels, and then press CTRL/CMD+D to drop the selection.

Only the edges of the cloud image are currently selected. Blurring them will help us to blend multiple cloud images together seamlessly.

4 A new clouds layer

Select the 'Background' layer and ALT/OPT-click on ▣ to create a new layer called "left clouds" just above it. Press Z and ALT/OPT-click twice on the image to zoom out to 50%.

Apply Filter > Render > Clouds and select Edit > Transform > Perspective. In the Options bar set W to 50% and drag the top left control into the top left corner of the image. Now set X to 0, drag the bottom middle control point over to the edge of the cloud (as shown) and release. Press ENTER twice to apply the transformation.

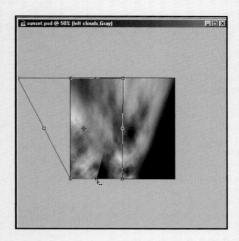

Press Z and click twice on the image to return the zoom to 100%.

The perspective clouds on the left side are complete.

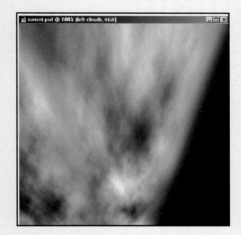

5 Balancing the clouds

ALT/OPT-click on ▣ to create a new layer called "right clouds". Press CTRL/CMD+F to reapply the Clouds filter, and SHIFT+CTRL/CMD+T to reapply the Perspective Transform. Select Edit > Transform > Horizontal Flip and press V to select the Move tool. Now SHIFT-drag the 'right clouds' layer sideways until it snaps to the right-hand edge of the image.

Transform a second clouds layer to add perspective and fill in the right side of the image. By filling in the edges, the clouds will soon look like they are disappearing towards the horizon.

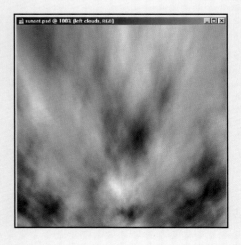

6 Resizing the image

Press SHIFT+CTRL/CMD+E to merge all that's visible into a single layer. Now select Image > Image Size, and in the Image Size dialog, uncheck Constrain Proportions. Change Height to 250 pixels and click OK to resize the image.

> *Stretching the image emphasizes the perspective of the clouds, giving the appearance of great depth.*

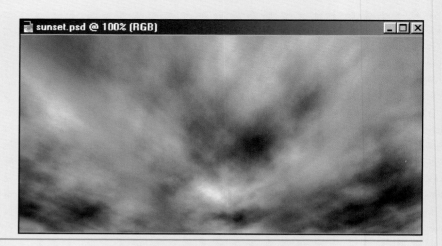

7 Inverting the image

Press CTRL/CMD+I to invert the color of the clouds – if you think the clouds don't look as good as they did before, hit CTRL/CMD+I again to change them back.

> *The sunset will look most realistic when there are relatively distinct clouds, as opposed to a large cloud area with holes in it. The first image is my original, and the second is its inverse. I decided that the original looks best, with a large cloud in the top right corner and a slightly smaller one on the right, so I left the clouds in their original state.*

8 Duplicating the layer

Now press CTRL/CMD+I to invert one more time, so the image looks like the clouds you *didn't* pick. Hold down ALT/OPT and drag the background layer onto the 🖺 button to create a duplicate layer named "clouds 2".

Open the Filter > Artistic > Film Grain window, and set Grain to 1, Highlight Area to 3, and Intensity to 3. Click OK to run the filter.

> Film Grain adds contrast to the edges of the clouds.

9 Adding more depth

Change the blending mode of the 'clouds 2' layer to Color Dodge, and then click on the background layer. Open the Filter > Distort > Spherize window. Select the 'Vertical only' mode, set the Amount to 100%, and click OK.

> The Spherize filter will create some variation and depth by shifting parts of the background layer to change the way it interacts with the 'clouds 2' layer.

10 Creating a levels adjustment layer

Re-activate the 'clouds 2' layer. Click the ◑ button on the Layers palette, and choose Levels. Click the Auto button on the Levels dialog, and then click OK.

> The levels adjustment layer maximizes the contrast of the two cloud layers.

SECTION 4: SKY

11 Adding color

Click the 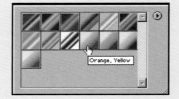 button again, and create a Gradient Map adjustment layer. In the Gradient Map dialog, click the button next to the gradient to open the list of preset gradients. Click the ⊙ button, and select `Pastels.grd` from the pop-out dialog. If asked whether to replace the current gradients with `Pastels.grd`, click OK. Double-click on the fourth gradient, "Yellow, Pink, Purple", and then click OK.

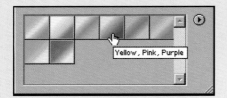

The Gradient Map adds dramatic colors to the sky, applying the yellow portion of the gradient to the darkest parts of the clouds, and the purple to the light areas.

12 Adding another gradient

Click on the 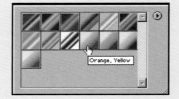 button to create a Gradient adjustment layer (*not* a Gradient Map adjustment layer). In the Gradient dialog, load the `Color Harmonies 2.grd` presets, select "Orange, Yellow", and click OK.

Change the blend mode of the 'Gradient Fill 1' adjustment layer to Soft Light.

Notice how the sky appears slightly brighter and more yellow near the horizon.

13 Creating the sun

Hold down ALT/OPT and click  on the Layers palette to create a new layer (on the top of the layer stack) named "sun". Press ALT/OPT+BACKSPACE to fill the layer with black, and set the blend mode to Color Dodge.

Use Filter > Render > Lens Flare with Brightness set to 100%, and select the 105mm Prime Lens Type. Click in the Flare Center box to pick where the sun should appear in the image, and click OK.

14 Blending in the sun

Press CTRL/CMD+U to open the Hue/Saturation dialog. Turn on Colorize and set Hue to 0, Saturation to -25, and Lightness to -50. Click OK.

Desaturating and darkening the 'sun' layer makes the effect more realistic.

The Finished Product

Variations and Applications

For some sunset variations, try changing gradients and blend modes, or adding buildings, mountains or other objects to the foreground.

In this example, the 'clouds 2' layer was set to use Screen mode to soften the clouds, and the Gradient adjustment layer was modified to use the "Purple, Yellow" gradient.

Here I made the clouds very dark and foreboding by setting the 'clouds 2' layer to Darken, changing the Gradient adjustment layer to use "Yellow, Pink, Purple", and then creating another copy of the layer and setting it to Hue mode. Finally, I created a third Gradient adjustment layer to add a band of red at the horizon.

Nebulae

Sunsets are nice to gaze at on Earth, but wouldn't it be cool to make the outer space version of a sunset? The nebulae that are produced in this section can be tiled seamlessly, and you can combine this technique with the following one ('Starfields') to make a complete universe.

1 Creating a cloud base

Press CTRL/CMD+N to create a new RGB document, 512x512 pixels, with a white background. Hit OK and press SHIFT+CTRL/CMD+S to save it as nebulae.psd. Press D to reset the default colors and run Filter > Render > Clouds. Press SHIFT+CTRL/CMD+L to run Auto Levels.

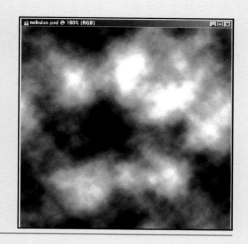

The image dimensions are both multiples of 256, so the Clouds filter will produce a tileable pattern.

2 Texturing the clouds

Hold down ALT/OPT, and drag the background layer onto the 🔲 button to create a duplicate of the clouds, "clouds 2". Select Filter > Distort > Spherize and then set Amount to -50% and Mode to 'Horizontal only'. Click OK.

For some additional distortion, open the Filter > Distort > Twirl dialog. Set the Angle to 50 degrees and click OK. Now select Filter > Artistic > Film Grain. Set Grain to 1, Highlight Area to 0, Intensity to 5, and click OK.

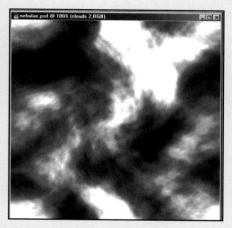

The 'clouds 2' layer emphasizes the shape that will become the nebula. Twirling the clouds slightly adds a subtle sense of spinning. Film Grain is used in this instance to emphasize edges of the nebula's structures.

3 Changing the blend

Double-click the 'clouds 2' layer in the Layers palette to open the Layer Style window. Change the blend mode to Darken, deselect the Channel B checkbox (under Advanced Blending), and click OK.

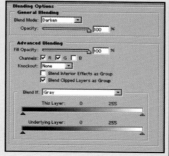

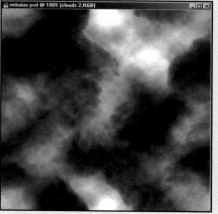

The 'clouds 2' layer is now darkening the background, and is not blending its blue channel. This adds a nice blue glow around some of the nebula's edges.

4 Reducing the size of the nebula

Click the 🖉 button on the Layers Palette, and select Levels. In the Levels dialog, click the Auto button, set the second of the Input Levels to 0.60, and click OK.

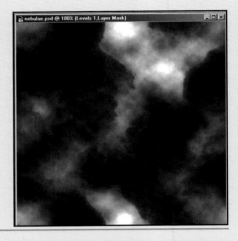

> *Shifting the image's middle brightness reduces the size of the nebula and leaves more room for empty space and stars.*

5 Adding color

Click the 🖉 button and create a Gradient Map adjustment layer. In the Gradient Map dialog, click the button next to the gradient to open the list of preset gradients. Click the ⊙ button, and select `Pastels.grd` from the pop-out dialog. Double-click the "Yellow, Pink, Purple" preset, and then turn on Reverse. Click OK to close the window, and change the blending mode of the Gradient Map layer to Hard Light.

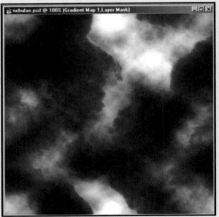

> *The Gradient map makes the brightest parts of the clouds yellow, and the darkest portions purple. Using Hard Light with the Gradient Map layer allows the blue areas to shine through.*

6 Creating a new levels adjustment layer

Click the 🖉 button and create another Levels adjustment layer at the top of the layer stack. In the Levels dialog, click Auto, set the middle input level to 0.50, and click OK.

Change the layer's blend mode to Multiply and its opacity to 50%.

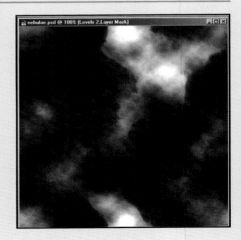

> *Moving the brightness midpoint with Levels modifies the sharpness of the nebula's edges.*

The Finished Product

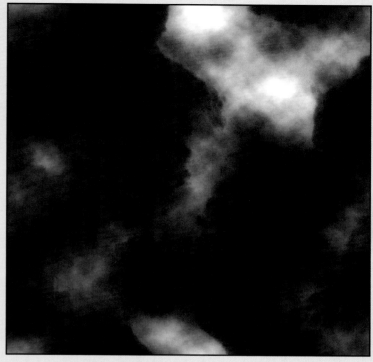

Variations and Applications

Because many of the nebula's adjustment layers and apply mode settings remain dynamic, it's easy to make quick variations without making permanent changes to the layers.

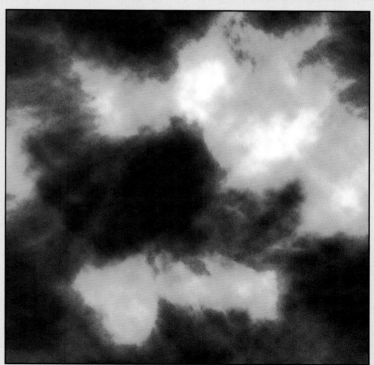

Starfields

Creating a field of stars is quick and easy with Photoshop. This technique can be done on its own, or as a continuation of the Nebulae technique demonstrated in the previous section. If you just want stars, start with a new RGB document, 512x512 pixels, with a white background.

1 Creating the sky

Open nebulae.psd and save it as stars.psd. Now ALT/OPT-click on 🔲 to create a new layer called "stars". Press ALT/OPT+BACKSPACE to fill the space with black. Use Filter > Noise > Add Noise with Amount set to 30%, Gaussian distribution, and Monochromatic checked. Click OK to apply.

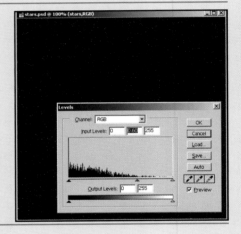

Add Noise fills the area with randomly spaced pixel-sized dots.

2 Differentiating the stars

Press CTRL/CMD+L. Set the middle input level to 0.60 and click OK.

The brightest dots remain bright, but others are now dimmer.

3 Adding a layer mask

Click the 🔲 button on the Layers palette to create a layer mask. Press D to set the default colors and apply Filter > Render > Clouds.

Open up the Levels dialog again with CTRL/CMD+L. In the Levels dialog, press Auto, and drag the middle input level slider (the gray triangle) over to the left until the dimmer stars fill back in to a desired brightness. Click OK to close Levels.

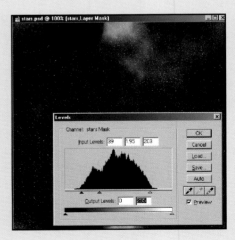

Adjusting the levels in this way brightens the stars.

4 Blending the stars

Change the blending mode of the stars layer to Screen.

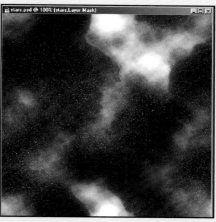

> *When set to Screen, the stars will be "added" to the layer underneath. If you started with the Nebulae technique, you should now see a large population of stars around the nebula.*

5 Adding brighter stars

Select the Airbrush tool by pressing J and open the drop-down Brush dialog from the Options bar. Click on the ⊙ button and select Assorted Brushes.abr from the pop-out menu. Select the 'Crosshatch 1' brush.

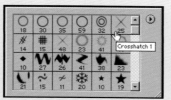

In the Layers palette, click on the 'stars' layer thumbnail to reactivate the layer's contents.

Press X to change the foreground color to white, and then add stars by clicking on the canvas.

> *Adjust the paintbrush's opacity to add variation to the stars.*

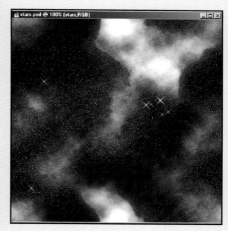

6 Adding a sun

Create a new layer, and set its blend mode to Screen. Press CTRL/CMD+BACKSPACE to fill the layer with black. Select Filter > Render > Lens Flare, set a position for the sun, set its Brightness to 50% and Type to '105mm Prime', and hit OK.

Press CTRL/CMD+L to open the Levels dialog and hit Auto. Press CTRL/CMD+1 to select the Red channel, and set the second of the Input Levels to 1.3 to simulate a red corona.

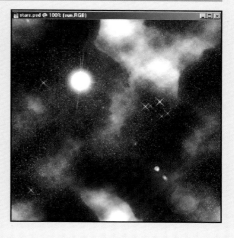

SECTION 4: SKY

The Finished Product

Variations and Applications

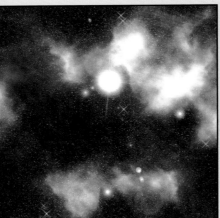

SECTION 5: TEXT

5.1 Plastic

5.2 Metal

5.3 Reptile

5.4 Bubble

5.5 Stained Glass

SECTION 5: TEXT

Plastic

By combining the use of Lighting Effects and Levels, we can create a very realistic, very flexible plastic effect.

1 Creating our 'X' base

Press CTRL/CMD+N to create a new RGB image, 250 pixels by 250 pixels, 72 pixels/inch, with a white background. Then hit SHIFT+CTRL/CMD+S and save it as `plastic.psd`.

Open the Swatches palette and click on the appropriate cell to set the foreground color to blue.

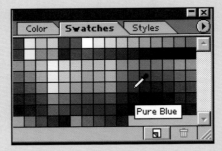

Press T to select the Type tool and specify Times New Roman in the Options bar with a font size of 300pt. Click in the bottom left corner of the image, and type in a capital "X". Press V to select the Move tool and drag the letter to the center of the image.

2 Stroking the 'X'

Click on the 🌑 button at the bottom of the Layers palette, and pick Stroke from the pop-up menu. In the Layer Style dialog, change Size to 2px, and Color to Black (just click on the color box and drag the cursor to the bottom left of the Color Picker).

Now click OK to confirm your settings.

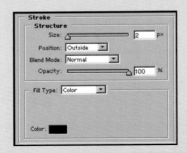

3 Blurring the 'X' channel

CTRL/CMD-click on layer 'X' to make a selection based on its contents.

Open up the Channels palette and ALT/OPT-click on 🔲 to make a new channel called "bevel". Hit ALT/OPT+BACKSPACE to fill the selection with the current foreground color (white – see below).

Use Filter > Blur > Gaussian Blur three times, with Radius set to 3, 2, and 1 each time respectively.

Use CTRL/CMD+SHIFT+I to invert the selection and hit DELETE.

Note that when working with Channels, the default colors are reversed (compared to those seen when working with Layers), so the default foreground color is white.

4 Creating the 'plastic' layer

Switch back to the Layers palette and ALT/OPT-click on its ⬛ button to create a new layer called "plastic".

Once again, CTRL/CMD-click on layer 'X' to make a selection based on its contents.

Hit D to select default colors, and ALT/OPT+BACKSPACE to fill the selection with the current foreground color (black).

Use Filter > Render > Lighting Effects with the default style, but with Texture Channel set to 'bevel' and properties modified as shown opposite:

Click OK to confirm. Finally, set the blend mode for the 'plastic' layer to Screen.

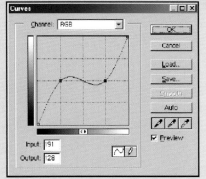

> *Use a 'map' of the bevel – stored in one of the channels – to apply the lighting effects to a very specific area within the text.*

5 Adjusting the curves

Press CTRL/CMD+M to call up the Curves control panel. Click and drag the RGB curve into the shape shown, so as to sharpen the highlights a little.

6 Adding glow

Once again click on the 🔘 button at the bottom of the Layers palette, and this time select Inner Glow from the pop-up menu.

Set the Choke to 30% and click on the color box to specify a light blue color as per the following settings:

> *This gives a little extra brightness and adds highlights to the plastic effect.*

79

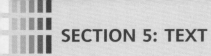

SECTION 5: TEXT

The Finished Product

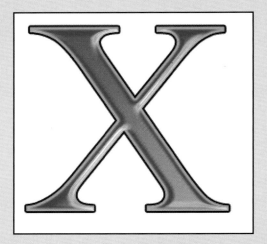

Variations and Applications

Metal

This example will show you one way to give your text a heavy metallic look. The basic technique behind this effect has been in use since as far back as Photoshop 3, but usually took a great deal more work to accomplish in the past.

1 Creating our 'M' base

Press CTRL/CMD+N to create a new RGB image, 225 pixels by 225 pixels, 72 pixels/inch with a white background. Save it as metal.psd.

Press T to select the Type tool and specify Arial Black in the Options bar with a font size of 200pt. Click in the bottom left corner of the image, and type in a capital "M". Press V to select the Move tool and drag the letter to the center of the image.

In the Layers palette, right-click (CTRL-click for Mac users) on the new type layer 'M' and select Rasterize Layer from the pop-up menu that appears. Then check the box next to 🔲 to lock the transparency of pixels in this layer.

> *Using the letter "M" in large, bold type, using a fairly simple font, gives us more scope to add our own fine details within the metal effect.*

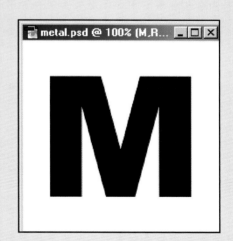

2 Adding a gradient

Open the Swatches palette, and click on a light gray cell to set the foreground color.

Now ALT/OPT-click on a dark gray cell to set the background color.

Press G to select the Gradient tool, and make sure that Linear Gradient is selected in the Options bar (shown below).

Click and drag from top to bottom of the letter "M" to make a nice vertical fade from light to dark.

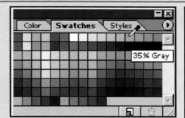

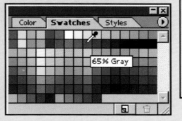

3 Adding a 'bevel' layer

ALT/OPT-click on the 🔲 button to create a new layer, which you should call "bevel".

CTRL/CMD-click on the 'M' layer, and select Edit > Fill. Specify 50% Gray in the Fill dialog, hit OK, and press CTRL/CMD+D to drop the selection.

Finally, use the dropdown menu at the top of the Layers palette to change the new layer's blend mode to Overlay.

SECTION 5: TEXT

4 Adjusting the curves

CTRL/CMD-click the 'bevel' layer. Use the arrow keys to nudge the selection 4 pixels to the left and 4 pixels up.

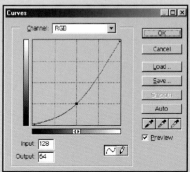

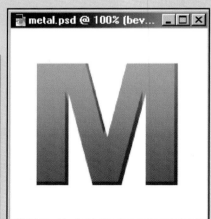

Press SHIFT+CTRL/CMD+I to invert the selection, and CTRL/CMD+M to call up the Curves dialog. Click on the center of the graph you see here, and drag it about three quarters of the way to the bottom.

CTRL/CMD-click the 'bevel' layer to reselect it, and this time nudge it 4 pixels to the right and 4 pixels down. Once again, hit SHIFT+CTRL/CMD+I and CTRL/CMD+M. This time, drag the center of the line upwards.

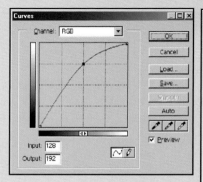

We could have used the Bevel and Emboss layer effect here to achieve a fairly similar end result. While that approach may be slightly quicker, this one gives us more flexibility, providing us with a separate effects layer onto which we can add further effects.

5 Creating the 'texture' layer

ALT/OPT-click the ▣ button. This will create a new layer, which you should call "texture" and drag to the top of the layer stack. With this layer still selected, CTRL/CMD-click on the 'M' layer to make a selection based on its contents.

Once again, select Edit > Fill with 50% Gray, and hit OK. Then select Filter > Noise > Add Noise with Amount set to 8.3, Distribution to Gaussian, and Monochromatic checked. Hit OK and press CTRL/CMD+D to drop the selection.

6 Modifying the texture

Select Filter > Blur > Motion Blur and set Angle to 30°, Distance to 40.

Now select Filter > Sharpen > Unsharp Mask and set Amount to 200%, Radius to 2.0, and Threshold to 0.

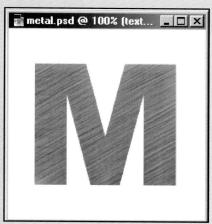

7 Sharpening the texture

Press R, and use SHIFT+R to cycle through the Blur/Sharpen/Smudge tool set until you activate the Sharpen tool △.

Open the Brush dropdown in the Options bar, and select the Spatter 25 pixels brush (as shown in the screenshot).

In the Options bar, set Pressure to 20%. Now use this brush to create areas of increased sharpness on the 'texture' layer.

Finally, set the blend mode to Overlay.

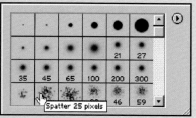

8 Adding scuffs

ALT/OPT-click on 🔲 to create a new layer called "more scuffs". Press D to ensure that black is selected as the foreground color, and select the same brush as used in the last step.

Paint some dark scuffmarks onto the 'more scuffs' layer, set its blend mode to Overlay and use Filter > Sharpen > Sharpen.

Now select the 'texture' layer and press CTRL/CMD+F to reapply the Sharpen filter.

9 Adding depth

Double-click on the original text layer 'M' to open up the Layer Styles dialog, and click the Stroke tab. Set Color to black and Size to 1px to add a thin black line around the text.

Now select Drop Shadow from the list of effects, and press OK to accept the default settings.

Just as a finishing touch, click and Alt/Opt-click on the Swatches palette to pick light and dark gray as foreground and background colors respectively. Press G to select the Gradient tool, and hold down SHIFT while you click at the bottom of the image and drag to the top.

The Finished Product

Variations and Applications

Try using dull orange (RGB: 106, 77, 70) scuffmarks to add a rusty appearance to the text.

Reptile

I bet you never knew that Photoshop had a built-in filter for creating reptilian skin effects – it's called Stained Glass! With just a few modifications and a little magic with bevels and layer modes, the reptile in your text will appear!

1 Creating the 'R' base

Hit CTRL/CMD+N to create a new RGB image (350px by 350px, with a white background) and SHIFT+CTRL/CMD+S to save it as reptile.psd.

Press T to select the Type tool, and use the Options bar to set the font to Georgia, 400pt. Select pure green from the Swatches palette, add a capital "R" to the image, and click the ✓ button in the Options bar to confirm. If necessary, press V and use the Move tool to center it.

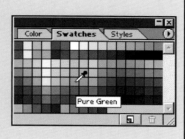

Now right-click (CTRL-click on a Mac) on the new type layer 'R' and select Rasterize Layer.

2 Creating scales

Open the Channels palette and ALT/OPT-click on the button to create a new channel called "scales".

Select Filter > Texture > Stained Glass, and in the Stained Glass dialog set Cell Size to 3, Border Thickness to 2, and Light Intensity to 4.

Press CTRL/CMD+L to bring up the Levels dialog, and set the first of the Input Levels to 100. Hit OK and press CTRL/CMD+I to invert the channel.

Adjust levels to get rid of the highlight in the middle of the stained glass texture.

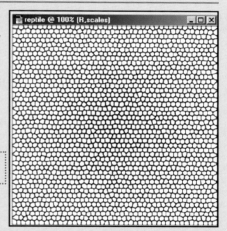

3 Selecting the scales

Call up the Layers palette, and CTRL/CMD-click on the 'R' layer. Then press SHIFT+CTRL/CMD+I to invert the selection.

Back on the Channels palette, select the 'scales' channel and press DELETE.

Finally, CTRL/CMD-click the 'scales' channel to form a selection based on the scales themselves.

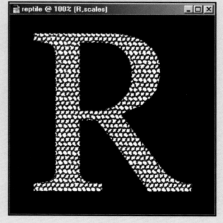

4 Creating the 'reptile' layer

On the Layers palette, ALT/OPT-click on the 🔲 button to create a new layer called "Reptile 1".

Select a darker green foreground color, and hit ALT/OPT+BACKSPACE to fill the selection with it. Now press CTRL/CMD+D to drop the selection.

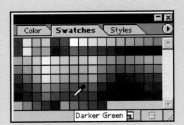

5 Adding bevel

With the 'Reptile 1' layer still selected, click on the 🔘 button at the bottom of the Layers palette, and select Bevel and Emboss from the pop-up menu.

Specify the settings shown. You should only need to change Size to 4px, Highlight Mode to Color Dodge, and Shadow Mode to Multiply (with 50% Opacity).

Click OK to confirm.

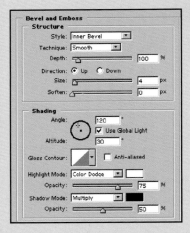

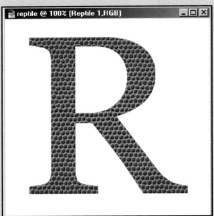

6 Randomizing the texture

Press E to select the Eraser tool, and pick the 'Spatter 39 pixels' brush from the brush menu on the Options bar.

Use rough strokes to erase sections of the 'Reptile 1' texture, leaving most remaining close to the edges.

> *A naturalistic look of reptilian skin really starts to show through when we use brush strokes to randomize the scaly texture.*

7 Creating a new layer

Ctrl/Cmd-click on the 'scales' channel.

Switch to the Layers palette, and Alt/Opt-click on  to create a new layer called "Reptile 2". Drag it in between layers 'R' and 'Reptile 1'.

Set the foreground color to yellow and press Alt/Opt+Backspace to fill the selection with it.

8 Duplicating effects

Drag the 'Bevel and Emboss' layer effect from 'Reptile 1' to 'Reptile 2', so that the effect we defined in Step 6 is applied to the new layer.

Next click on 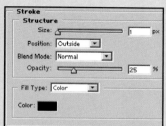 and select Stroke, changing Size to 1px, Opacity to 25%, and Color to black.

Hit OK to confirm.

9 Creating another layer

Alt/Opt-drag the 'Reptile 2' layer onto the button to create a duplicate layer called "Reptile 3" and Ctrl/Cmd-click on the new layer.

Click on the Swatches palette to set the foreground color to orange, and press Alt/Opt+Backspace to fill the current selection with that color.

Now press E to select the Eraser (with the same brush set as was used in Step 6) and use it to remove irregular areas of the 'Reptile 3' layer so that plenty of yellow scales show through from the 'Reptile 2' layer as shown.

The Finished Product

As a finishing touch, you may like to add a suitable background and add a Drop Shadow effect to the original type layer 'R'. I've used a couple of images from earlier in the book — earth.psd and water.psd (using Color Dodge at 70% opacity) — for the background shown here.

Variations and Applications

In this example, I've just added a background texture and some more beveled scales around the edges of the image.

Here, I've left both foreground and background green, and added an outer glow to the text.

In this case, I created one set of scales on top of another.

Bubble

This technique will demonstrate how you can make a smooth transition from normal 'squared' text to 'rounded' text, and then use a combination of bevels, highlights, textures, and layer modes to put the 'bubble' into 'Bubble Text'.

1 Creating the bubble base

Press CTRL/CMD+N to create a new RGB image, 400 pixels wide, 120 pixels high, 72 pixels/inch, with a white background. Then hit SHIFT+CTRL/CMD+S and save it as bubble.psd.

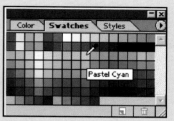

Press T to select the Type tool, and select Arial Black, 100pt from the Options bar. Click on the Swatches palette to set the foreground color to a light blue color like the one shown opposite.

Click inside the image and type "Bubble", and hit the ☑ button in the Options bar to confirm. Press V and use the Move tool to center the text. Right-click (CTRL-click on the Mac) on the text layer and select Rasterize Layer.

2 Creating the 'rounded' channel

CTRL/CMD-click the 'Bubble' layer to make a selection based on the text it contains.

On the Channels palette, ALT/OPT-click on the ⬚ button to create a new channel called "rounded".

Press D (to set default colors) and ALT/OPT+BACKSPACE (to fill with the current foreground color) to fill the selection with white. Press CTRL/CMD+D to drop the selection.

Now select Filter > Blur > Gaussian Blur and set the Radius to 4.

3 Adjusting the levels

Press CTRL/CMD+L to open the Levels dialog.

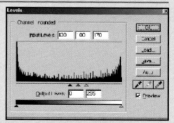

Set minimum and maximum input levels to 130 and 170 respectively, and press OK.

> The closer together these values are, the sharper the text's edges become.

SECTION 5: TEXT

4 Adding bevel

CTRL/CMD-click the 'rounded' channel to make a selection.

Switch to the Layers palette and ALT/OPT-click on the ▣ button to create a new layer called "round text". Now press ALT/OPT+BACKSPACE to fill the selection with the same light blue as we used before.

You can now delete the 'Bubble' layer – just drag it onto the 🗑 button.

Click 𝒇. and select Bevel and Emboss from the pop-up menu. In the Layer Style dialog, change Size to 4px, Soften to 6px, Highlight Mode to Color Dodge, and Shadow Mode to Overlay.

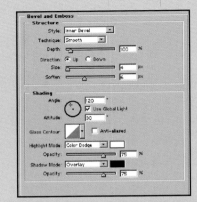

5 Adding glow and stroke

With the Layer Style dialog still open, click on Inner Glow and set Color to sky blue (RGB Value 0, 217, 225) and Choke to 4%.

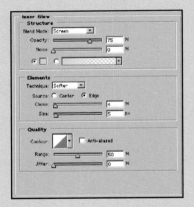

Now click on the Stroke entry at the very bottom, and set Size to 2, Opacity to 75, and Color to a darker blue to signify an outline. Click OK.

6 Adding texture

On the Layers palette, ALT/OPT-click the 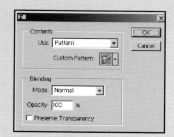 button to create a new layer and call it "texture".

Select Edit > Fill to call up the Fill dialog. Change the Use setting to Pattern, and specify the Water Bubbles pattern (the first pattern in the list by default).

Click OK to confirm.

Press CTRL/CMD+U to call up the Hue/Saturation dialog, pull down the Saturation level to -50 (to dull the color a little) and hit OK.

Now change the 'texture' layer's blend mode to Overlay, press CTRL/CMD+D to drop the selection, and CTRL/CMD+E to merge the layer down into the 'round text' layer.

7 Separating the letters

Select the 'round text' layer and use the Marquee tool (M) to drag a selection around the first 'B'. Press CTRL/CMD+C to copy it to the clipboard, and CTRL/CMD+V to paste it into a new layer. Reselect the 'round text' layer and repeat for each of the other letters until you have six new layers (numbered 1 through 6) that contain one letter each.

Make sure the 'round text' layer is active, and for each new layer in the Layers palette, click on the empty box just to the right of the 👁 image so that a small 🔗 image appears, indicating a linked layer.

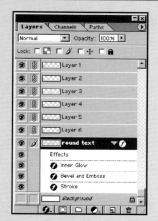

Right-click (CTRL-click for Macs) on the 'round text' entry and select Copy Layer Style from the pop-up menu that appears. Call up the menu again, and select Paste Layer Style to Linked.

Drag the original 'round text' layer onto the 🗑 button to delete it, and click on all the 🔗 images to unlink the layers.

8 Adding bubbles

On the Layers palette, ALT/OPT-click on the ![] button to create a new layer, and call it "bubbles".

Press M to select the Rectangular Marquee tool, and SHIFT+M to switch over to its counterpart, the Elliptical Marquee tool. Click on an empty part of the canvas and SHIFT-drag to make a small circular selection. Click on the Light Cyan entry in the Swatches palette to set the foreground color, and press ALT/OPT+BACKSPACE to fill the selection.

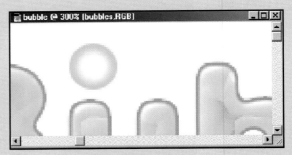

Now use Select > Modify > Contract to contract the selection by 3 pixels and CTRL/CMD+ALT/OPT+D to feather it by 3 pixels. Press DELETE to get rid of the bubble's center, and CTRL/CMD+D to drop the selection.

Press B to select the Paintbrush tool, D to set the default colors, and X to exchange them. Now select a soft 3 pixel brush from the Options bar and paint in a small highlight in the top left corner of the bubble.

9 Making final adjustments

Now drag the 'bubbles' layer onto the ![] button to duplicate the layer. Press V to select the Move tool, and use this to drag the duplicate bubble into another part of the image. Do this a few times until you have five or six bubbles distributed around your text.

You should now have roughly eleven layers (not counting 'Background') making up the image. Select each one in turn, and use the Transform tool (CTRL/CMD+T) to adjust the position, size, and orientation of the letters and bubbles so that they look as if they could be floating. You may also like to rearrange the order of layers in the layer stack.

Finally, with the 'Background' layer active, use Edit > Fill to fill it with the Water Bubbles pattern we used in Step 6 and apply Filter > Blur > Gaussian Blur with a Radius of 3.0.

The Finished Product

Stained Glass

As the Reptile Type effect demonstrated earlier, the Stained Glass filter provides us with a very effective way to generate random meshes. Let's see if it lives up to its name – we'll use it to make some text look like it's actually made of stained glass.

1 Creating the text base

Press CTRL/CMD+N to create a new RGB image, 375 pixels by 150 pixels, at 72 pixels/inch, with a white background. Then hit SHIFT+CTRL/CMD+S and save it as stained glass.psd.

Press T to select the Type tool. Select 72pt, Arial Black from the Options bar, and click on the Swatches palette to select red as the foreground color.

Type "Stained" into the image, click the ☑ button in the Options bar to confirm, and use the Move tool (V) to center it.

Now right-click (CTRL-click on a Mac) on the new type layer 'Stained' and select Rasterize Layer.

2 Creating the 'frame' layer

Hold down ALT/OPT while you drag the 'Stained' entry in the Layers palette onto 🔲 and give the duplicate layer the name "frame". Now turn off the 'Stained' layer's visibility by clicking on the 👁 button to the left of its Layer palette entry.

CTRL/CMD-click on the 'frame' layer to make a selection based on its contents. Select Menu > Modify > Contract to contract the selection by 2 pixels and press DELETE. Now press CTRL/CMD+D to drop the selection.

3 Creating the stained glass texture

Call up the Channels palette and ALT/OPT-click on the 🔲 button to create a new channel called "mesh".

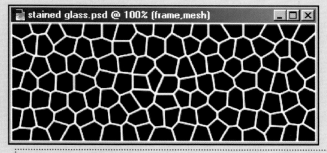

Press D to ensure that the default colors are set, and select Filter > Texture > Stained Glass. In the dialog, set Cell Size to 10, Border Thickness to 4, Light Intensity to 3, and click OK to confirm.

Press CTRL/CMD+L to call up the Levels dialog, set the first of the Input Levels to 50 and hit OK.

We create a stained glass texture in the 'mesh' channel, and adjust levels to get rid of the central highlight.

4 Adding the mesh texture

CTRL/CMD-click on the 'mesh' channel to make a selection based on its contents.

Call up the Layers palette and ALT/OPT-click on  to create a new layer called "grid". Press ALT/OPT+BACKSPACE to fill the selection with red.

Now CTRL/CMD-click on the 'stained' layer, press SHIFT+CTRL/CMD+I to invert the area of selection and press DELETE.

Press CTRL/CMD+E to merge the 'grid' layer down onto 'frame', and CTRL/CMD+D to drop the selection.

5 Adding bevel and stroke

Check the ▢ box at the top of the Layers palette and select Edit > Fill with 50% Gray.

Click on  and pick Bevel and Emboss from the pop-up menu. In the Layer Style dialog, change Size to 2px and Soften to 0px. Click on the Stroke entry in the left-hand list of Layer Effects, and set Size to 1px, Color to black, and Opacity to 40%.

6 Perfecting the stained glass texture

Select the 'stained' layer and CTRL/CMD-click on the 'frame' layer to select the frame area. Press DELETE to remove areas of color that are covered by the frame – you shouldn't see any change unless you hide the 'frame' layer.

Press CTRL/CMD+D to drop the selection, and G followed by SHIFT+G to select the Paint Bucket tool. Make sure that 'Contiguous' is checked on the Options bar, and ▢ is checked for this layer in the Layers palette.

Click on the Swatches palette to set the foreground color to green, and click on a few of the red patches within the letters to change their colors. Repeat with two or three other fairly vivid colors.

Finally, select Filter > Noise > Add Noise (with Amount set to 10%, Distribution to Gaussian, and Monochromatic checked) to add some noise to the colors.

7 Adding highlights

CTRL/CMD-click on 'Stained'. ALT/OPT-click on ▣ to create a new layer called "highlights" and drag it to the top of the stack.

Select > Modify > Contract by 2 pixels, and then Select > Feather by 2 pixels.

Press D to set default colors, press CTRL/CMD+BACKSPACE to fill with white and CTRL/CMD+D to drop the selection.

Set the layer's blend mode to Luminosity with 70% opacity.

8 Modifying the background

Open up the Channels palette, and CTRL/CMD-click on the 'mesh' channel.

Return to the Layers palette and select the 'Background' layer. ALT/OPT-click on the ▣ button to create a new layer called "mesh" just above the background, and press ALT/OPT+BACKSPACE to fill the selected area with black.

Click on the bar labeled 'Effects' (just under the 'frame' entry in the layer stack) and drag it onto the 'mesh' layer to copy across the layer effects.

9 Coloring the background

Click and ALT/OPT-click on the Swatches palette to set foreground and background colors to Pale Warm Brown and Darker Warm Brown respectively.

ALT/OPT-drag the 'Background' layer onto the ▣ button to create a new layer called "clouds". Apply Filter > Render > Difference Clouds and press CTRL/CMD+F to reapply the filter roughly ten times more.

Now CTRL/CMD-click on the 'mesh' layer and press DELETE. Finally, set the opacity for both 'clouds' and 'mesh' layers to 50%.

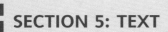

SECTION 5: TEXT

The Finished Product

Variations and Applications

Text effects such as the ones in this chapter are useful to accentuate the message that you are trying to get across with your use of lettering. Best of all, these techniques aren't just confined to working on text – there's nothing to stop you applying them to all kinds of different shapes!

Here, I changed the background and added a little more noise and some extra highlights.

SECTION 6: DEPTH

6.1 Wire Mesh

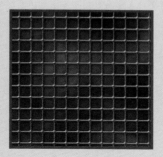

6.2 Corrugated Pipe

6.3 Vine-Covered Text

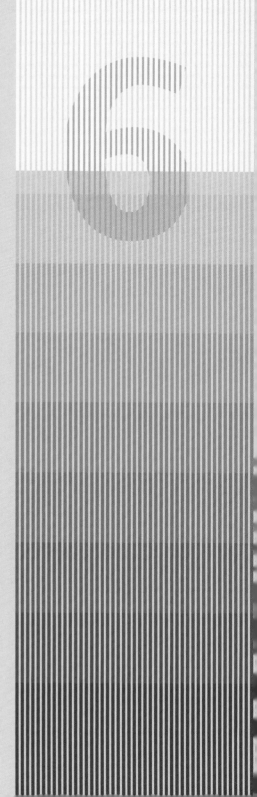

SECTION 6: DEPTH

Wire Mesh

Have you ever wanted to put someone or something behind bars? Or make an iron mesh pattern suitable for heavy-duty doors and fences? Here's how you can do it.

1 Creating a mesh square

Press CTRL/CMD+N to create a new RGB image, 30x30 pixels, with a white background. Press D to reset the default colors, then press ALT/OPT+BACKSPACE to fill the layer with black.

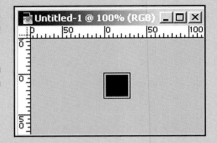

Press CTRL/CMD+A to select all, and then choose Select > Modify > Border. Choose a border width of 2 pixels, and click OK. Press CTRL/CMD+BACKSPACE to fill the selection with white. Then, press CTRL/CMD+D to drop the selection.

> *We now have a white box pattern that will create a mesh when repeated. The width of the border can be changed to adjust the thickness of the wires, and the size of the square can be adjusted for a larger or smaller mesh*

2 Modifying the mesh

Go to Filter > Blur > Gaussian Blur. Select a radius of 2 pixels, and click OK. Press CTRL/CMD+L to bring up the Levels dialog. Put in the values below to sharpen the edges, and hit OK.

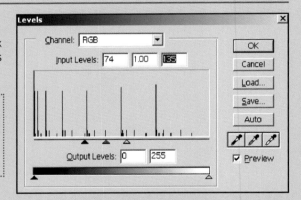

> *Using levels, in conjunction with Gaussian Blur is a great way to create sharp, smooth edges. The blur smoothes out the edges in the corners, which will create a slight bulge where wires intersect. Using levels re-sharpens the edges to create a smooth shape with slight curves in the corners.*

3 Defining the Mesh pattern

Press CTRL/CMD+A to select the canvas, and go to Edit > Define Pattern. This feature will add the currently selected image to Photoshop's list of patterns. Enter a name of "wire mesh" and click OK.

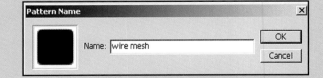

> *The wire shape is now "saved" internally. You can close the original document.*

4 Starting the mesh image

Open `meshbackground.psd` from the download folder to use as the base for our mesh image.

> *The image has a size of 390x390, so the 30x30 wire pattern will repeat 13 times in each direction.*

5 Creating the pattern channel

Hold down ALT/OPT and click the ⬚ button on the Channels palette to create a new channel called "wire map". Go to Edit > Fill and under Contents, select "Pattern". Click the Custom Pattern button, select the wire mesh pattern and click OK.

> *A repeating mesh pattern now fills the wire map channel.*

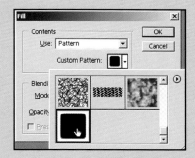

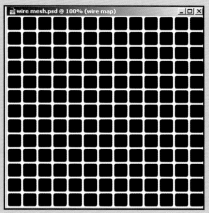

6 Creating the 'wires' layer

Hold down ALT/OPT and click the New Layer button ⬚ on the Layers palette to create a new layer called "wires".

In the Channels palette CTRL/CMD-click the 'wire map' channel to load its contents as a selection.

Choose Edit >Fill, select "50% Gray" as the fill contents, and click OK. Press CTRL/CMD+D to drop the selection.

> *The 'wires' layer now contains a solid gray mesh pattern.*

7 Adding shadow

Click the Add Layer Style button  on the Layers palette, and choose Drop Shadow. In the Layer Style dialog, set the Opacity to 35% and leave the other settings at their default values.

Drop Shadow gives depth to the image by making the wire mesh appear above the background.

8 Adding highlights

In the left pane of the Layer Style dialog, click on the Bevel and Emboss button. When the settings show in the right pane, change Technique to "Chisel Hard", Shadow Opacity to 100%, and select the 'Cove – Deep' Gloss Contour.

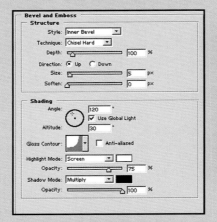

These Bevel/Emboss settings give the wire mesh a sharp, high-contrast highlight.

9 Adding more highlights

Now click on the Inner Shadow button to call up its settings in the right-hand pane. Change Blend Mode to Screen, Color to white and Opacity to 50%. Deselect 'Use Global Light', and set the Angle to -90°. Change Distance to 2px and Size to 1px.

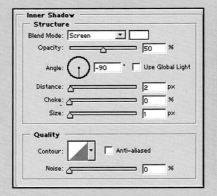

Using Inner Shadow in this way actually creates a highlight on the bottom edges of the wires to emphasize a second light source.

Notice how in step 9 we use the Inner Shadow effect to create a highlight. You'll find that Layer Styles can be wonderfully surprising when you start using them for purposes other than their names imply. Bevels can create glowing effects, Outer Glow effects can create borders, and shadows can be interchangeable with highlights. As always, keep experimenting!

10 Adding stroke

Enable Stroke, and bring up its settings. Change Size to 1px, Opacity to about 45%, and change the stroke color to black.

Click OK to close the Layer Style window.

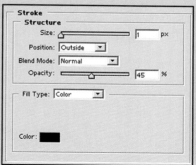

Adding a subtle stroke gives the wire mesh more contrast and definition around the edges.

11 Color Variations

Click the New Fill/Adjustment Layer button  on the Layers palette, and choose Hue/Saturation. Turn on Colorize, set Hue to 16, Saturation to 25 and Lightness to -30, and click OK.

Press CTRL/CMD+G to group the adjustment layer with the previous layer, to limit the effect of the adjustment to the opaque areas of the wire mesh.

Press D to return to Photoshop's default colors, and then run Filter > Render > Difference Clouds. Press CTRL/CMD+F a few times to repeat the filter and add additional variation to the rust color. Then press SHIFT+CTRL/CMD+L to run Auto Levels.

A Hue/Saturation adjustment layer allows dynamic color changes in the wire mesh. This makes the highlights and shadows look more realistic, as they are not so consistent over the area of the image. The masked Hue/Saturation layer applies the rusty color to specific areas of the mesh.

12 Giving the rust texture

Go to Filter > Noise > Add Noise. Use an Amount of about 50%, with a Gaussian, Monochromatic Distribution, and click OK.

Adding noise to the rust's mask gives the wire mesh a rough appearance.

The Finished Product

Variations and Applications

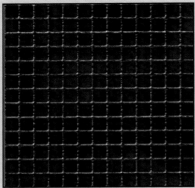

Here, I just ran Filter >Texture > Craquelure *with the default settings.*

In this case, I used Filter > Distort > Wave *(with 1 Generator of Type "Triangle", with Undefined Areas set to "Wrap Around".*

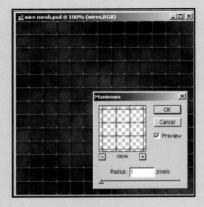

To get a more net-like effect, you can thin the wires using Filter > Other > Maximum *on the wire mesh layer.*

Alternatively, use Filter > Other > Minimum *to thicken the wires – now it's a heavy iron grate.*

Corrugated Pipe

To continue in the same vein, let's try a different kind of metal object – a corrugated pipe!

1 Beginning the pipe pattern

Press CTRL/CMD+N to create a new RGB image, with a white background, 300x15 pixels. Press CTRL/CMD+I to invert the image so that it is black.

Press M to select the Rectangular Marquee tool, and press SHIFT+M if the Elliptical Marquee tool is highlighted. Select about the middle one-third of the image, making sure your selection goes from top to bottom. Press CTRL/CMD+I to fill the selection with white. Then press CTRL/CMD+D to drop the selection.

> *This image is thin as it will be used as a repeatable pattern to create the pipe structure.*

2 Distorting the pattern

Go to Filter > Distort > Shear. In the dialog, click to create two points, and position them just as shown. Click OK.

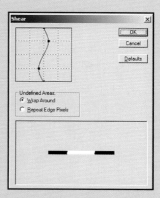

> *Shear is used here to create an alternating ridge in the white portion of the image, which will form a thin slice of pipe.*

3 Adding some detail

Choose Image > Rotate Canvas > 90 degrees CCW. Press the D key to load the default colors – black and white.

Select the Straight Line tool by pressing the U key. If another shape tool is highlighted, hold shift down and keep pressing U to cycle through the tools. On the Options bar, make sure that the third button "Create filled region" is pressed, and that the line tool is selected with no arrowheads enabled.

Select a Weight of 1 pixel, and check 'Anti-aliased'. Click and drag to draw a line to connect the "valley" in the upper-right to the "valley" in the lower-left.

> *The thin line separates the ridges of the corrugated pipe.*

4 Saving the pattern

Press CTRL/CMD+A to select the entire canvas, and then choose Edit > Define Pattern. Give the pattern the name "corrugated pipe" and click OK. The pipe pattern is now saved in Photoshop's internal list of patterns, so you can close this image window now.

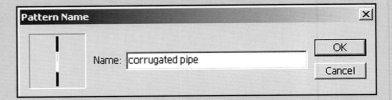

This pattern will form the structure of our pipe.

5 Creating the pipe channel

Open `pipebackground.psd` from the download folder.

On the Channels palette, hold down ALT/OPT and click the Create New Channel button, to create a new channel named "pipe map". Go to Edit > Fill, select 'Pattern', use the pop-up window to select the corrugated pipe pattern from the list, and click OK.

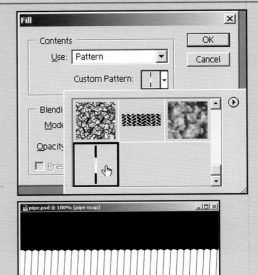

The filled pipe map channel contains the shapes of the pipe ridges.

6 Creating the pipe layer

CTRL/CMD-click on the 'pipe map' channel to load it as a selection.

Open the Layers palette and ALT/OPT-click on the button to create a new layer called "pipe". Now use Edit > Fill to fill the selection with "50% Gray", and press CTRL/CMD+D to drop the selection.

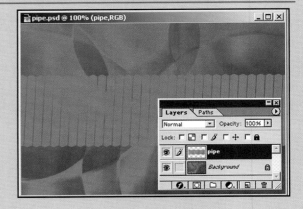

This creates the basic shape of the pipe.

7 Adding a Gradient overlay

Click the button on the Layers palette and select Gradient Overlay. Use the settings shown below.

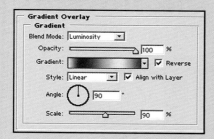

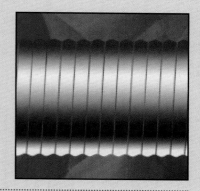

The Copper gradient used here is located in the default gradients preset. (You can load the default gradients by selecting the "Reset Gradients" option from within the gradient list view.)

Notice how the Luminosity Blend Mode results in a grayscale pipe, even though the gradient itself is copper-colored.

8 Adding bevel

Keep the Layer Style window up and continue by turning on Bevel and Emboss and bringing up its settings by clicking on the text. Enter the settings as shown.

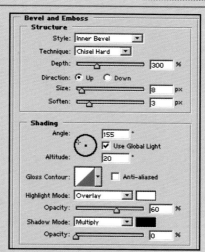

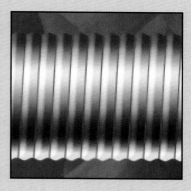

The Bevel/Emboss layer style adds a bright highlight to the left side of each pipe ridge.

9 Making the pipe solid

In the Layer Style window, turn on Stroke, and bring up its settings. Set Size at 1 pixel, and change the Color to a dark gray, using Red:100, Green:100, Blue:100.

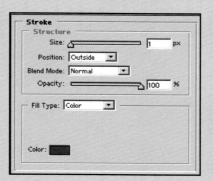

The Outside Stroke fills in the gaps between the ridges and makes a continuous pipe shape.

SECTION 6: DEPTH

10 Adding more realism

Enable Satin and bring up its settings view. Set the options as in the screenshot below.

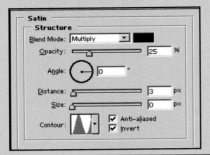

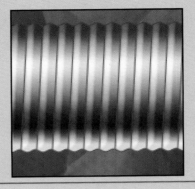

Satin creates interesting highlights and shadows and works by shifting and blurring the shape. Now the pipe has much more realistic highlights.

11 Adding Shadow

The final layer style we need is the standard Drop Shadow. Enable it and bring up its settings. Set them to the values shown below, and click OK.

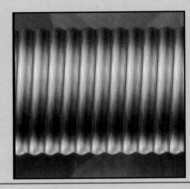

The Drop Shadow adds the illusion of depth between the pipe and the background image.

12 Creating an adjustment layer

Click the New Fill/Adjustment layer button to create a new Hue/Saturation adjustment layer. In the Hue/Saturation options, enable Colorize, enter the values shown below, and click OK.

This gives the pipe a rusty color.

13 Modifying the color.

Press the D key to revert to Photoshop's default colors. Go to Filter > Render > Difference Clouds Press CTRL/CMD+F a few more times to reapply the filter.

Select Filter > Noise > Add Noise, and when the dialog appears set Amount to 10%, with Monochromatic and Gaussian Distribution selected, and click OK.

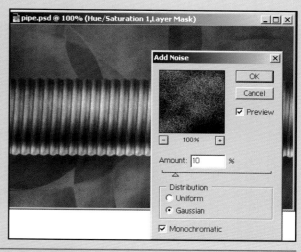

Applying the clouds filter adds variation to the hue/saturation adjustment layer to add complexity to the mask. Adding noise to the hue/saturation mask creates a rough texture among the rusty blemishes.

14 Limiting the effects of the new layer

CTRL/CMD-click the pipe layer to load its opacity levels as a selection. Go to Select > Modify > Expand, choose a value of 1 pixel to include the space between the ridges, and click OK.

Press CTRL/CMD+SHIFT+I to invert the selection, then press the DELETE key to clear the area. Press CTRL/CMD+D to drop the selection.

This limits the effects of the adjustment layer to the pipe itself.

15 Adjusting the levels

Finally, press CTRL/CMD+SHIFT+L to run Auto Levels on the mask.

Auto Levels alters a layer's brightness levels to ensure that the entire range of levels is used, from the darkest black to the brightest white. This makes the rusty blemishes stand out a little more.

The Finished Product

Variations and applications

Layer styles do most of the work needed to simulate the highlights, shadows, and depth. Due to the dynamic nature of the styles, if you rotate the pipe, layer styles such as gradients, light sources, and other aspects will not get transformed appropriately, and it won't look quite right. You can, however, link the adjustment and pipe layers together, and merge them, which will permanently render the dynamic effects to the pipe. Alternatively, you can choose Layer > Layer Style > Create Layers, and link all the related layers together before doing a transformation.

In this example, I added an opening at the end of the pipe, and made a few blurred duplicates to give a greater illusion of depth.

Here, I used distortion filters to give the pipes a more organic look.

Vine-Covered Text

Now that we've looked at a couple of realistic metal techniques, let's try something on the opposite end of the spectrum – something organic... something alive!

1 The text

Open up `vinetext.psd` from the download, and save it as `vines.psd`.

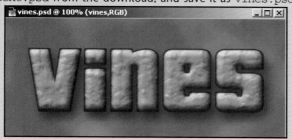

When you try this effect on your own text, ideally your text should be large and in a very heavy font weight.

2 Creating the vine map

Hold down the ALT/OPT button and click the New Channel button on the Channels palette, to create a new channel named "vine map"

Press D to load Photoshop's default colors, and run Filter > Render > Clouds.

Use Filter > Pixelate > Crystallize with a Cell Size of 30, and apply Filter > Stylize > Find Edges.

Press CTRL/CMD+I to invert the channel.

This makes the vine structures start to appear.

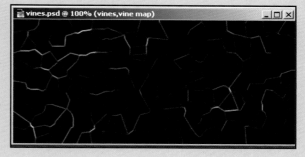

3 Emphasizing the edges

Select Image > Adjust > Threshold, set Threshold Level to 1, and click OK.

Now apply Filter > Blur > Gaussian Blur with a Radius of 2 pixels to get rid of jagged edges created by Threshold.

Press CTRL/CMD+L to open the Levels window. Set the first and last Input Levels to 75 and 130 respectively, and click OK.

Choose Filter > Distort > Ocean Ripple. Select a Ripple Size and Magnitude of 1. Click OK.

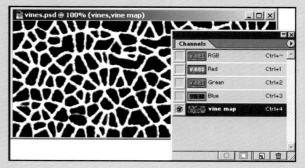

With small values, Ocean Ripple gives the vines just the right amount of distortion. The vine map channel is finished and ready for action!

SECTION 6: DEPTH

4 Selecting text

Back in the Layers palette, ALT/OPT-click on 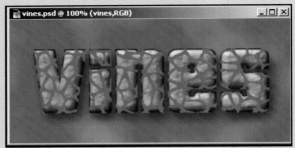 to create a new layer called "vines", and place it above the text layer.

With the new, blank layer active, CTRL/CMD-click on the text layer to load it as a selection, and use Select > Modify > Expand to expand the selection by 1 pixel.

Open the Channels palette and SHIFT+CTRL/CMD+ALT/OPT-click on the 'vine map' channel to load its *intersection* with the current selection.

Back in the Layers palette, make sure the vines layer is active and use Edit > Fill with '50% Gray' specified as the fill contents. Then press CTRL/CMD+D to drop the selection.

This gives the vines a base color.

5 Adding stroke

Bring the layer's Opacity down to 70%. Double-click the vines layer on the Layers palette to open the Layer Style window. Enter the settings as shown in the screenshot below.

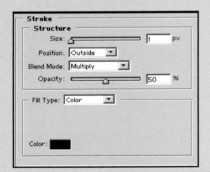

The Stroke gives the vines a more visible edge.

6 Changing the Color Overlay

Enable the Color Overlay style, set the color to R:24, G:126, B:0, and the Opacity to 70%.

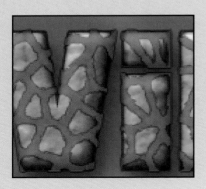

7 Adding Gradient Overlay

Enable Gradient Overlay and apply the settings below.

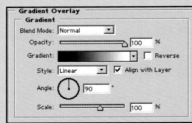

The Gradient Overlay makes the vines slightly brighter along the top of the text.

8 Adding depth

Enable Bevel and Emboss, and enter the values shown in the screenshot below.

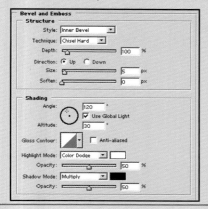

The Inner Bevel adds depth and emphasizes a light source in the upper-left.

9 Adding texture

Enable Texture and select the pattern, adjusting the settings as below.

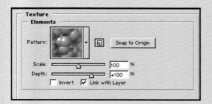

Adding a bevel texture like this one adds bumps and segments to the vines.

10 Adding slime

Enable Inner Glow and set the values to those in the screenshot below.

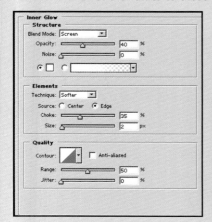

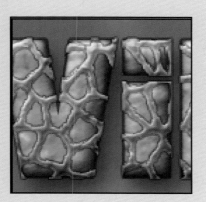

Inner Glow is used to add that necessary touch of "slime" to the vines.

111

SECTION 6: DEPTH

11 Make those vines shine

Enable Satin and apply the settings below.

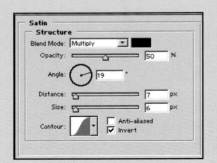

This emphasizes the shiny look of the vines.

12 Adding shadow

Enable Drop Shadow and set it to the values shown below.

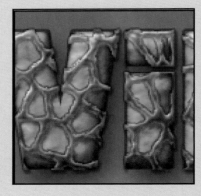

The Drop Shadow 'lifts' the vines off the surface of the text.

The Finished Product

SECTION 7: VOLUME

7.1 Metal Sphere

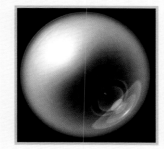

7.2 Disco Ball

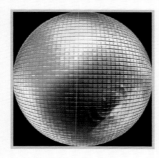

7.3 Textured Sphere

7.4 Textured Cube

Metal Sphere

Spheres have always been an area of great interest for designers – they are nice general-purpose design elements that can be used for buttons, logos, or simply to fill space and look cool. Here's a somewhat unlikely approach to simulating spherical highlights, shadows, and reflections.

1 A new document

Press CTRL/CMD+N to create a new RGB image, 500x500 pixels in size, with Contents set to "White". Press CTRL/CMD+I to invert the color of the background, and SHIFT+CTRL/CMD+S to save it as sphere.psd.

Now ALT/OPT-drag the 'Background' layer onto to create a duplicate layer called "sphere".

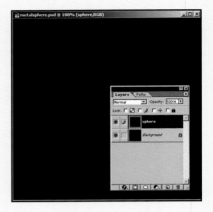

2 Beginning the sphere

Select Filter > Render > Lens Flare. Hold down ALT/OPT and click on the image thumbnail – set the coordinates to X:160, Y:160 and press OK to set the Flare center. Increase Brightness to 150%, select '50-300mm Zoom' and click OK.

This flare will form one of the sphere's highlights.

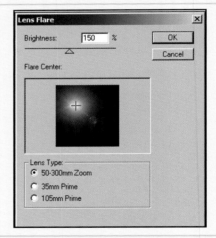

3 Adding another highlight

Press CTRL/CMD+SHIFT+L to run Auto Levels. Use Filter > Render > Lens Flare again, but this time with Lens Type set to '105mm Prime' and Brightness set to 100%.

The second lens flare adds additional refractions in the lower right part of the image.

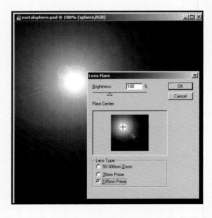

4 Blending the flares

Press SHIFT+CTRL/CMD+F to combine the output of the previously run filter (Lens Flare) with the image that existed before the filter was used. Select the Screen mode, and click OK.

5 Distorting the flares: part 1

Select Filter > Distort > Polar Coordinates, check the 'Polar to Rectangular' option, and click OK. Next, apply Image > Rotate Canvas > Flip Vertical.

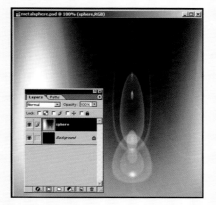

6 Distorting the flares: part 2

Select Filter > Distort > Polar Coordinates again. This time, select the 'Rectangular to Polar' option, and click OK.

The second use of Polar Coordinates "wraps" the image back into a circle. We can see our sphere beginning to take shape.

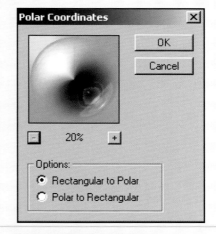

7 Adding guides

Press CTRL/CMD+R to show the rulers, and make the image window larger so you have a bit more space to work. Enable View > Snap and drag guides into the canvas area as shown opposite.

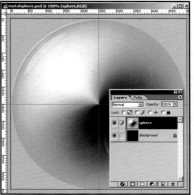

115

8 Selecting the point

Press M, SHIFT+M to select the Elliptical Marquee tool. Open the Info palette and SHIFT+ALT/OPT-drag a circle out from the center guides until it's about 200x200 pixels in size. Press CTRL/CMD+ALT/OPT+D, enter a Feather Radius of 30 pixels, and click OK.

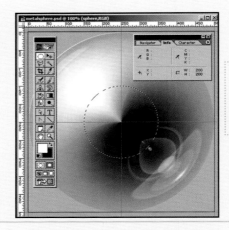

Using Feather with a large pixel radius creates a very soft edge for the selection.

9 Getting rid of the point

Apply Filter > Blur > Gaussian Blur with a Radius of 40 pixels.

With the Elliptical Marquee tool still in use, draw a new selection by dragging from the upper left corner of guides down to the lower right corner, creating a selection around the entire sphere. Press CTRL/CMD+SHIFT+I to invert the area of selection, and press DELETE to clear the background.

Press CTRL/CMD+D to drop the selection, followed by CTRL/CMD+H (to hide the guides) and CTRL/CMD+R (to hide the rulers).

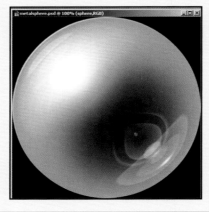

Gaussian Blur smoothes out the sharp point in the shape's center, so it looks like a real sphere.

10 Resizing the image

Press D to set the default colors, and X to reverse them. Use Image > Canvas Size to open the Canvas Size dialog, set Height and Width to 550 pixels, and click OK. The new space is filled with the background color, which should be black.

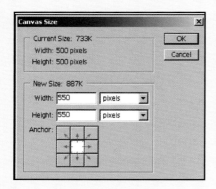

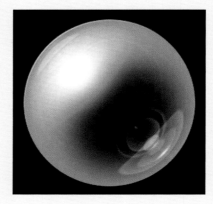

Use Canvas Size when you want to change an image's size without rescaling anything.

A little extra space around the edges makes it easier to focus on the sphere and not feel limited by the edges of the canvas.

11 Emphasizing the spherical effect

Double-click the 'sphere' layer to open the Layer Style window. Click Inner Glow to enable it and display its options. Change the Blending Mode to Multiply, Opacity to 75%, Size to 40px, and use a dark blue shade for the glow (R:39, G:84, B:157). Click OK.

The Multiply mode will always darken, so this Inner "Glow" style is actually acting more like a shadow.

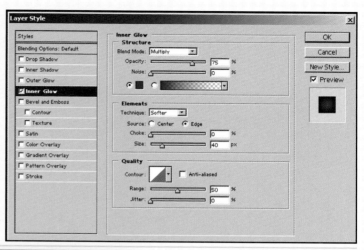

The Finished Product

Variations and Applications

Try altering the color and brightness distributions with a Levels adjustment layer, or by using Image > Adjust > Variations. Reflections can be added by overlaying an image on top of the sphere and using the Filter > Distort > Spherize filter.

To create this variation, I replaced the black background with an image, duplicated that image above the sphere (using the Overlay blend mode) and applied Filter > Distort > Spherize to distort the reflection. I then created a Levels adjustment layer (masked with the shape of the sphere) and used it to adjust the levels of the red, green, and blue channels until I achieved the desired bronze appearance. I finished it off by adding a Drop Shadow layer style to the 'sphere' layer.

117

Disco Ball

Here's a technique that builds on the last exercise to make something a little funkier.

1 A new document

Open up `sphere.psd` file from the last exercise, and save it as `disco.psd`.

Click on the 'sphere' layer, and press CTRL/CMD+L to open the levels dialog. Set the Input Levels to 0, 0.70, 200, and click OK.

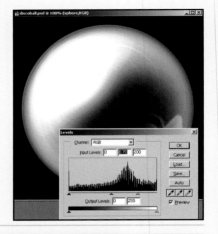

> *Use Levels to brighten the sphere's highlights.*

2 Changing the texture

Press D to load the default colors, and ALT/OPT-click on the ▢ button to create a new layer called "tiles". Go to Filter > Render > Clouds. Then use Filter > Blur > Gaussian Blur with a Radius of 20 pixels to smooth out the texture.

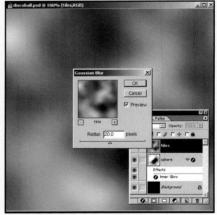

> *This applies a heavy blur to the output of the Clouds filter.*

3 Creating the tiles

Go to Filter > Texture > Patchwork. Use a Square Size of 6 and a Relief of 8, and click OK.

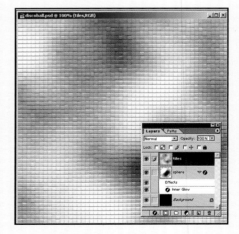

> *Patchwork provides the basis for the disco ball's mirrored tiles. A smaller Square Size will create the illusion of a larger disco ball.*

4 Wrapping the tiles

CTRL/CMD-click on the 'sphere' layer to load it as a selection. Then choose Filter > Distort > Spherize. Set Amount to 100%, leave the Mode as 'Normal', and click OK.

The tiled areas outside of the sphere aren't needed, so press CTRL/CMD+SHIFT+I to invert the selection, and press DELETE to clear the surrounding pixels. Press CTRL/CMD+D to deselect.

> *The mirrored tiles now appear to fit the shape of the sphere appropriately, and those outside the sphere have been removed.*

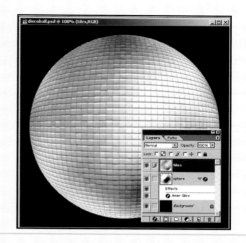

5 Adjusting the levels

Change the Opacity of the current layer to 50%. Press CTRL/CMD+L to open the Levels dialog. In the Levels window, press Auto, set the input levels to 0, 0.25, 255, and click OK.

> *Using Levels emphasizes the brighter mirror tiles.*

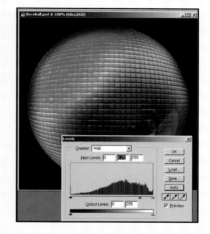

6 Adding more highlights

Repeat steps 2 to 4 again, this time naming the new layer "tiles 2". When you've completed the steps, including the use of Clouds, Gaussian Blur, Patchwork, and Spherize, your sphere should look like the one opposite.

> *We create a new layer from scratch so that the random effect produced by the clouds filter isn't an exact duplicate of the original.*

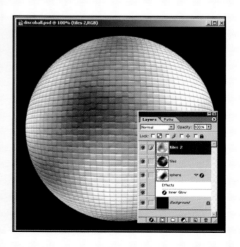

119

7 Emphasizing the new highlights

Choose Edit > Transform > Flip Vertical. Change the 'tiles 2' blending mode to Color Dodge, and bring the Opacity down to 70%. Open the Levels dialog by pressing CTRL/CMD+L. Set the input levels to 0, 0.35, 255, and click OK.

Using Levels emphasizes some of the brighter highlights.

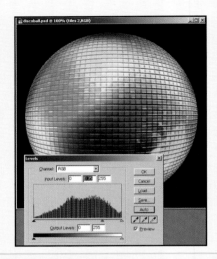

8 Creating a blue shine

As a final touch, click on the ⬤ button in the Layers palette, and select Inner Glow. Double the size of the glow, change its Blending Mode to "Hard Light" to make the blue glow more intense, and click OK.

This adds a colorful blue shine to the ball.

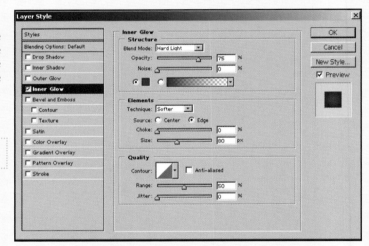

The Finished Product

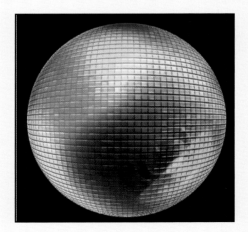

Variations and Applications

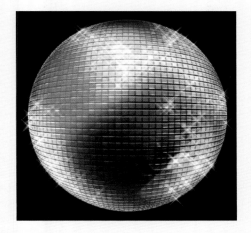

To get this effect, I created a new layer at the top of the layer stack and used the Paintbrush tool to paint in some star-shaped highlights (as demonstrated at the end of the Starfield technique in Section 4) for a more shiny appearance.

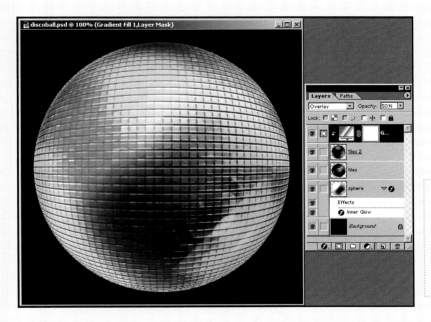

In this example, I created a Gradient fill layer, with the Chrome gradient preset selected. I grouped it with the 'tiles 2' layer, and set its mode to Overlay at 50% opacity. The gradient gives the impression of a horizon being reflected in the sphere.

Textured Sphere

Due to the plethora of slick features in Photoshop, there are a number of ways you could create realistic shading to simulate a sphere – from filters like Lighting Effects, to using Bevel/Emboss layer styles, to distorting a lens flare (see the Metal Sphere technique in this chapter). For this example, I'm going to demonstrate using a radial gradient to accomplish the effect. While this technique will work with any texture, I will use the planet texture from section 1 to make a sweet looking 3D world.

1 A new document

Open the `nebulae.psd` file from the download folder (or your own copy if you've worked through Section 4).Save it as `globe.psd`.

> *I darkened the nebula image so it won't distract*
> *from the real subject – the planet.*

2 Creating the 'sphere' layer

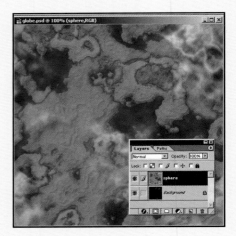

ALT/OPT-click on ⬛ in the Layers palette to create a new layer called "sphere", and open `planet.psd` from the download folder (or use your own copy from the example in Section 2).

Copy (CTRL/CMD+A, CTRL/CMD+C) and paste (CTRL/CMD+V) the planet texture into the new 'sphere' layer.

> *This texture will form the surface of our planet.*

3 Selecting a circle

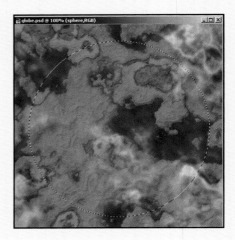

Hold down SHIFT and press M until the Elliptical Marquee tool is highlighted. Holding down the SHIFT key again, drag from the upper-left corner of the canvas down to the lower right to create a large circular selection like the one opposite.

> *Holding down the Shift key while dragging*
> *constrains the marquee to a perfect circle.*

4 Creating the sphere

Select Filter > Distort > Spherize. Keep the default settings (Amount: 100%, Mode: 'Normal') and click OK. Press SHIFT+CTRL/CMD+I to select the inverse. Then press the DELETE key to clear the surrounding texture, and then CTRL/CMD+D to drop the selection.

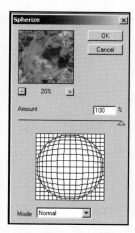

Spherize magically warps the texture as if it were wrapped on a sphere.

Proof that the Earth can be flat and round.

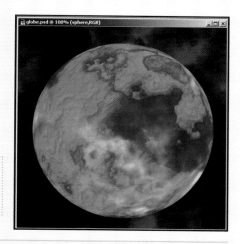

5 Sharpening the detail

Use Filter > Sharpen > Unsharp Mask with an Amount of 150% at 1 pixel to get back some of the detail that has been lost round the edges during the distortion.

The Unsharp Mask can improve almost any blurry image.

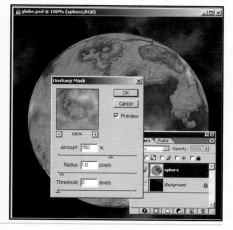

6 Adding some haze

Double-click the 'sphere' layer to open the Layer Style window. Turn on Inner Shadow, and click its name to bring up the shadow options. Change Color to a bright blue, Angle to -60 degrees, Choke to 25%, and Size to 50px, and click OK.

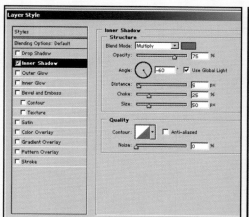

The haze around the planet's edge is subtle, but it emphasizes the depth of the sphere.

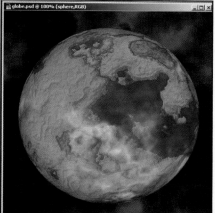

SECTION 7: VOLUME

7 Adding another layer

Hold down ALT/OPT and click the 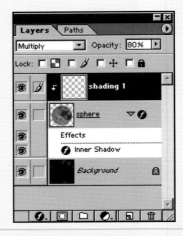 button on the Layers palette to create a new layer above the sphere, called "shading 1". Change its blending mode to Multiply, and its opacity to 80%. Then press CTRL/CMD+G to add the layer to the sphere's clipping group.

8 Adding shadow

Press G to select the Gradient tool. On the tool options bar at the top of the Photoshop window, select a white-to-black, radial gradient, as shown below.

Pick a point on the sphere to place the highlight, a little to the upper-left of center. Click and drag the mouse from that point, across the middle of the sphere, and release it on its opposite edge.

> *The gradient is applied with bright white at the point where we clicked, fading out to black, where we stopped dragging and released the mouse button.*

9 Varying the shadow

Press CTRL/CMD+M to open the Curves dialog. Click the line in the diagram a couple of times to add control points. Drag the points to move them into positions similar to those shown below and click OK.

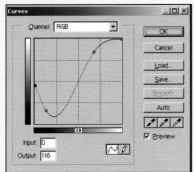

> *The leftmost point, which has been moved up, is used to create a second highlight where the darkest shadows used to be. This planet must have two suns in its system...*

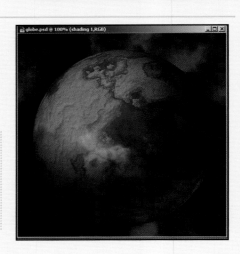

10 Adding another layer

Holding down the ALT/OPT key, drag the 'shading 1' layer onto the New Layer button on the Layers palette, and rename the layer "shading 2". Set its blending mode to Screen and its opacity to 30%.

We will use the 'shading 2' layer to intensify the main highlight.

11 Adjusting the threshold

Choose Image > Adjust > Threshold. Set Threshold to 225 and click OK.

Threshold converts the layer to a sharp-edged white-on-black highlight at the specified threshold level.

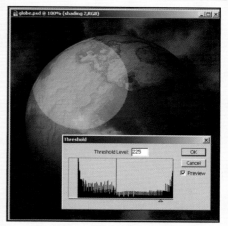

12 Blurring the highlight

Go to Filter > Blur > Gaussian Blur. Select a Radius of 20 pixels, and click OK.

With a heavy blur applied, you'd never guess that two separate highlights had been used.

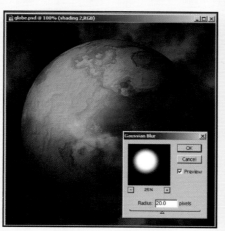

The Finished Product

Textured Cube

In this example, I'll demonstrate how to create a cube, smooth its corners and edges, and position images on its faces with realistic shading.

1 The basis of our image

Open `circles.psd` from the download folder. Hold down ALT/OPT and click the New Layer button on the Layers palette, to create a new layer called "cube". Save as `cube.psd`.

2 Creating the cube

Go to Filter > Render > 3D Transform. When the filter window appears, select the Cube Tool by clicking the button with the cube icon. Then drag the mouse in the work area to "draw" a cube.

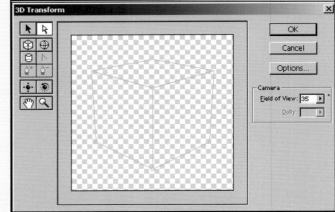

> *The green lines show the outline of the cube in relation to the canvas. The checker pattern indicates that the current layer is empty and transparent apart from the cube.*

3 Solidifying the cube

Press R to activate the Trackball Tool, and rotate the cube (by dragging the cursor around the work area) until all three faces are solid in color. You can use the Pan and Dolly controls to fine-tune the cube's placement. Then click the Options button. Set both Resolution and Anti-aliasing to 'High'. Click OK to close Options and then OK again to apply the 3D transformation.

> *The filter works by distorting the image, so nothing will happen by default because the layer is empty. However, the hidden sides of the cube become opaque if they are rotated into view.*

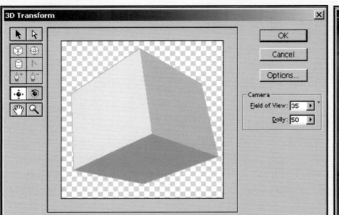

4 Adding guides

To help with the mapping of textures onto the cube's faces, we need to place an intersection of guides at each of the cube's seven visible corners. Choose View > Show Rulers if they are not already visible. Drag guides out from the horizontal and vertical rulers: each point should have two guide lines – one horizontal, and one vertical, as shown opposite.

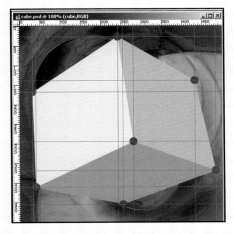

The red circles in this figure are highlighting the seven visible corners of the cube. Notice how two guides are placed for each point.

5 Rounding the corners

On the Layers palette, with the cube layer active, enable "Lock transparent pixels" by clicking the leftmost checkbox.

Then go to Filter > Blur > Gaussian Blur. Set the Radius to 5 pixels and click OK.

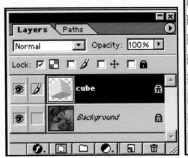

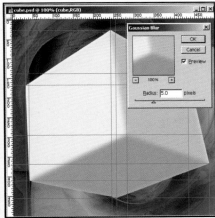

Because the cube's transparency is locked, Gaussian Blur doesn't soften the cube's outer edges.

6 Creating a new layer

Click on the background layer in the Layers palette to reactivate it. Hold down Alt/Opt and click the New Layer button to create a layer, named "rounded cube", that sits between the cube and the background image. Press D to reset to the default colors, and then press Alt/Opt+Backspace to fill the layer with black. Click on the cube layer to re-activate it, and then press Ctrl/Cmd+E to merge it with the rounded cube layer.

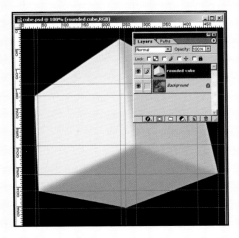

The cube layer is now gone – only the rounded cube and background layers remain.

7 Smoothing the edges

Bring up Filter > Noise > Dust & Scratches. Set the Radius to 15 pixels, and click OK.

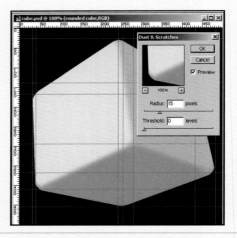

> *As the radius gets bigger, the rounded edges get smoother.*

8 Bringing the background back

Press W to select the Magic Wand Tool. In the Tool Options bar, set Tolerance to 15, and make sure that Anti-aliasing is on.

Click in the black area to select the layer content surrounding the cube. Press the DELETE key to clear the area, then CTRL/CMD+D to deselect.

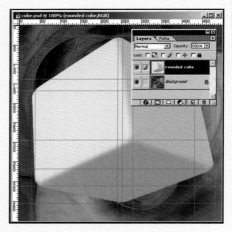

> *After deleting the surrounding black area, the background image is visible once again.*

9 Placing our images

Hold down the ALT/OPT key and create a new layer above the rounded cube layer called "cube face 1". Open eagle.psd from the download folder and copy and paste the image into 'cube face 1'. Change the blending mode to Overlay. Make sure View > Snap is turned on, then go to Edit > Transform > Distort. A bounding box appears around the image, with control points in its corners. Drag the corner points to the guide intersections that encompass one of the cube faces. Press ENTER to confirm the distortion.

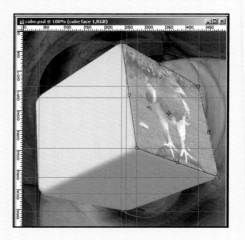

> *The Distort feature positions the image's corner points at those around a cube face, using the guides to snap.*

10 Scaling the image

Next, press CTRL/CMD+T to enter Free Transform mode. In the Options bar, change the width and height values to 95%. Click the checkmark button on the Options bar to confirm the change.

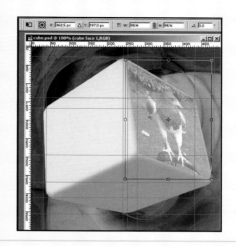

> *Scaling the image down a bit keeps the cube's corners visible.*

11 Sharpening the image

Open Filter > Sharpen > Unsharp Mask. Set Amount to 50% and Radius to 1 pixel for minor sharpening. Click OK.

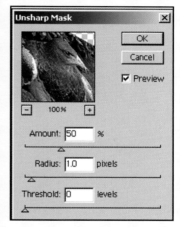

> *After distorting an image, it's usually a good idea to re-sharpen it to restore any lost detail.*

12 Rounding the corners

CTRL/CMD-click the current layer to load its opaque areas as a selection. Use Select > Modify > Smooth with a Sample Radius of 8 pixels. Press CTRL/CMD+SHIFT+I to select the inverse, DELETE to clear, and CTRL/CMD+D to deselect.

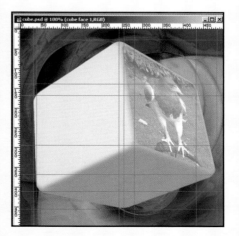

> *The image's corners have been rounded to fit the cube better.*

13 Filling the other faces

Repeat steps 9 through to 12 to create the other two cube faces, calling the new layers "cube face 2" and "cube face 3". I used the same bird for all three faces, but altered each to be a different color. Press CTRL/CMD+H to hide the guides and CTRL/CMD+R to hide the rulers as they are no longer needed.

The shading on the cube remains realistic thanks to the use of the Overlay mode. For example, the blue bird image was placed on the brightest cube face, and its appearance still reflects that. .

14 Intensifying the colors

Although the shading on the cube is preserved, the pictures look washed out. Change the blend mode of 'cube face 1', ' cube face 2' and 'cube face 3' to Multiply to intensify the colors, and bring the Opacity down to 70%.

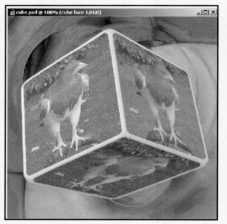

15 Adding bevel

Double-click on 'cube face 1' to bring up the Layer Style dialog. Click on Bevel and Emboss to bring up the settings, and change the values as shown in the screenshot opposite.

This adds more depth to the cube face.

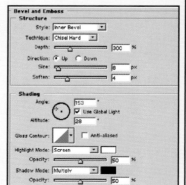

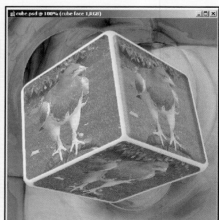

16 Adding glow

Click on Outer Glow to bring up the settings, and change the values as shown in the screenshot opposite.

This enhances the appearance of 3D.

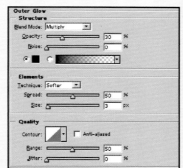

17 Adding stroke

Click on Stroke to bring up the settings, and change the values as shown in the screenshot opposite. Click OK.

This defines the edges of the picture.

18 Copying the effects to the other layers

Click on the Effects layer under 'cube face 1' and drag it upwards. Release it directly under 'cube face 2'. This duplicates the effects to the 'cube face 2' layer. Repeat this to copy the effects to the 'cube face 3' layer.

Now all the faces of the cube have identical effects applied.

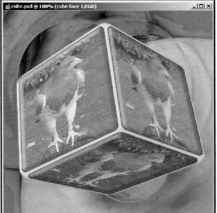

19 Adding shadow to the cube

Double-click on 'rounded cube' to bring up the Layer Style dialog. Click on Drop Shadow to bring up the settings, and change the values as shown in the screenshot opposite.

This makes the cube stand out from the background a little more.

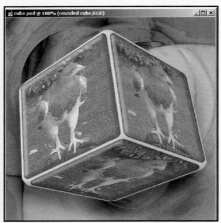

20 Stroking the cube

Click on Stroke to bring up the settings, and change the values as shown in the screenshot opposite. Click OK.

The stroke addds a final bit of definition to the cube.

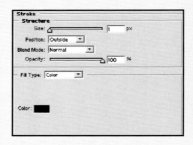

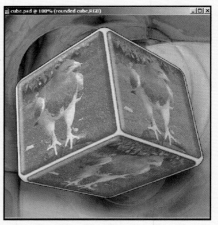

The Finished Product

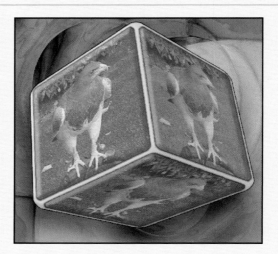

SECTION 8: INTERFACES

8.1 Round Interface

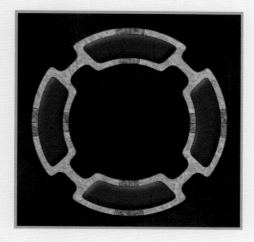

8.2 Advanced Interface Templates

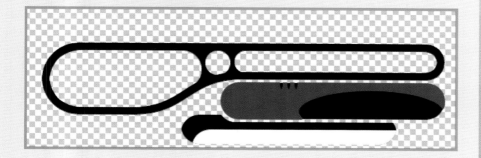

Round Panel Interface

Cool web interfaces have become increasingly popular as the web increases in popularity and cheap access to high bandwidth grows. Aside from creating buttons and wires (which we'll look at shortly) creating an eye-catching interface often boils down to creating an interesting shape.

Part 1 – The Basic Shape

1 Creating the 'Round Panel' document

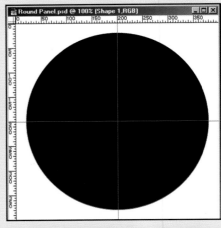

Press CTRL/CMD+N to create a new RGB document that is 360 pixels by 360 pixels at 72 pixels/inch, with a white background. Press SHIFT+CTRL/CMD+S and save it as Round Panel.psd.

Hit D to set default colors, and CTRL/CMD+R to view the rulers. Click in the left ruler and SHIFT-drag out a guide to 180 pixels across. Click in the top ruler and SHIFT-drag out another guide to 180 pixels down.

Press U (and SHIFT+U if necessary) to select the Ellipse tool. Click on the intersection of the guides and SHIFT+ALT/OPT-drag to the corner of the image, until the marquee just touches the edges. Select Layer > Rasterize > Layer.

Now select Image > Canvas Size, set Width and Height to 400 pixels, and hit OK.

2 Removing the middle of the panel

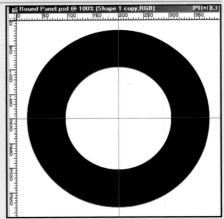

Drag the 'Shape 1' layer onto the ⬜ button to create a temporary duplicate. Press CTRL/CMD+T, set both W and H (in the Options bar) to 58% and hit ENTER twice to apply the transformation.

Press CTRL/CMD+I to invert the color of the layer.

3 Breaking up the ring

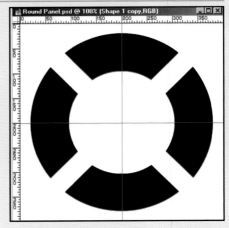

Drag the 'Background' layer onto the ⬜ button to create a temporary duplicate, and drag it to the top of the layer stack. Press CTRL/CMD+T, set W to 10%, and hit ENTER twice to apply the transformation.

Drag the 'Background copy' layer onto ⬜ . Press CTRL/CMD+T, set ◸ to 90%, and hit ENTER twice. Press CTRL/CMD+E to merge down onto 'Background copy'. Press CTRL/CMD+T again, set ◸ to 45%, and hit ENTER twice.

CTRL/CMD-click on the 'Background copy' layer. Open the Channels palette and ALT-click on ⬜ to create a new channel called "cross", and press ALT/OPT+BACKSPACE to fill the selected area with white.

Return to the Layers palette and make sure 'Background copy' is active. Press CTRL/CMD+E to merge down it onto 'Shape 1 copy'.

4 Making an inner ring

ALT/OPT-drag 'Shape 1' onto the New Layer button 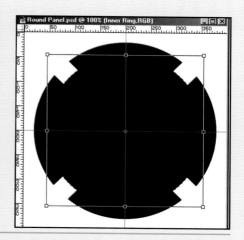 to create another duplicate called "Inner Ring", and place the new layer at the top of the layer stack. Press CTRL/CMD+T, set both W and H to 86%, and hit ENTER twice to apply the transformation.

5 Hollowing out the inner ring

Duplicate 'Inner Ring' and press CTRL/CMD+I to invert colors. Press CTRL/CMD+T, set both W and H to 84%, and hit ENTER twice to apply the transformation.

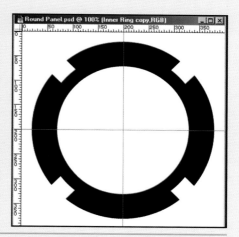

6 Merging the layers

Click on the 'Inner Ring' Layer palette entry and then CTRL-click on 'Inner Ring copy'. Press DELETE and then drag 'Inner Ring copy' onto the 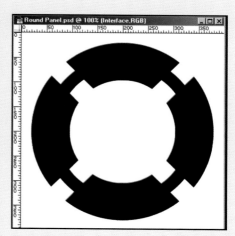 button at the bottom of the palette. Press CTRL/CMD+D to drop the selection, CTRL/CMD+H to hide the guides, and SHIFT+CTRL/CMD+E to merge all visible layers.

Finally, hold down ALT/OPT and double-click on the one remaining entry in the Layers palette – rename it "Interface".

Part 2 – Round Corners

We now have a fairly interesting shape on which to base our round panel, but some of the corners or edges are a little hard edged. Here's an effect you can use to make the shape softer.

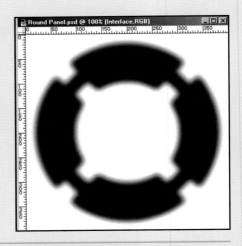

1 Blurring the edges

Select Filter > Blur > Gaussian Blur, set the Radius to 6 pixels, and hit OK to apply.

> *The amount of Gaussian Blur used here has a significant effect on the appearance of the finished product.*

2 Leveling all the grays

Press CTRL/CMD+L to open the Levels dialog. Set the first and last Input Levels to 45 and 70 respectively and hit OK.

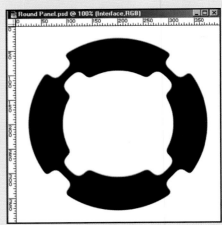

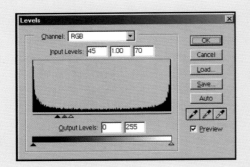

3 Pulling the shape off the background

Press CTRL/CMD+A to select all, and CTRL/CMD+C to copy the Interface image onto the clipboard.

Open the Channels palette and ALT/OPT-click on 🔲 to create a new channel called "Interface". Press CTRL/CMD+V to paste in the shape we've produced, and CTRL/CMD+I to invert its colors.

Back in the Layers palette, press DELETE to empty the 'Interface' layer, followed by CTRL/CMD+ALT/OPT+5 and ALT/OPT+BACKSPACE to put our shape back in – only without the white background!

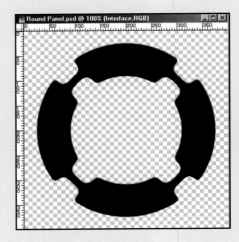

Variations

Try out other some Input Levels to see how they affect the overall appearance.

Settings like 215, 240 will make the corners round, but make the overall shape very fat.

On the other hand, settings such as 10, 20 will give a much thinner variation.

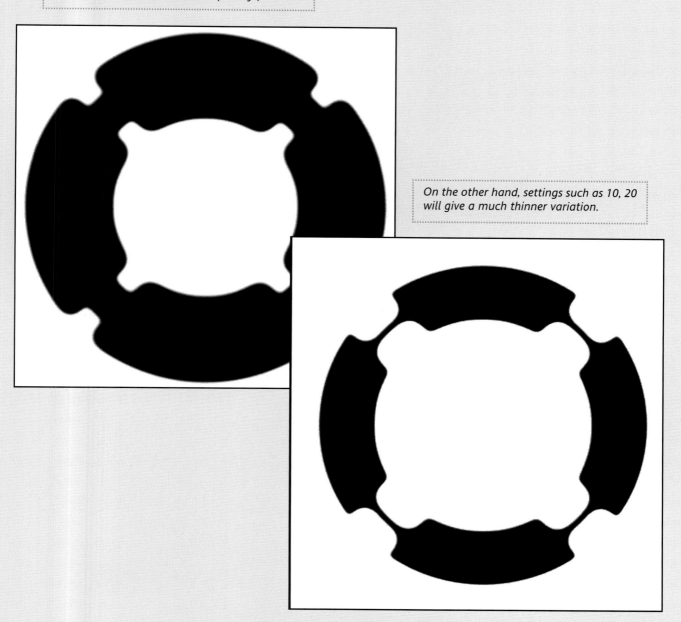

Part 3 – Creating Insets

We're now going to combine the techniques we've seen so far to create some nice inset regions on our interface.

1 Creating inset shapes

Open the Channels palette and ALT/OPT-drag 'cross' onto 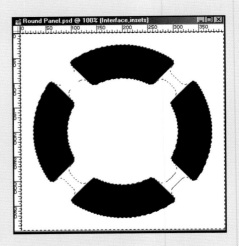 to create a duplicate channel called "insets".

Use Filter > Blur > Gaussian Blur with a Radius of 6. Now press CTRL/CMD+L to open the Levels dialog, set the Input Levels to 45, 1.00, 70, and hit OK.

CTRL/CMD-click on 'Interface', press SHIFT+CTRL/CMD+I to invert the area of selection, and ALT/OPT+BACKSPACE to fill the current selection with white.

> *Our insets are now the same shape as the thicker portions of the Interface.*

2 Trimming down the insets

Press CTRL/CMD+D to drop the selection, and apply Filter > Blur > Gaussian Blur with a Radius of 8.

Press CTRL/CMD+L to open the Levels dialog, set the Input Levels to 15, 1.00, and 25, and hit OK to apply.

Finally, Press CTRL/CMD+I to invert colors.

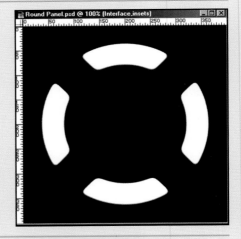

> *Now we have our button shapes. As we see will see in a moment, these buttons fit nicely within the overall interface shape.*

3 Checking your channels

If everything's gone to plan, your Channels palette should now look like this.

> *If not, go back and check that you've completed all the above steps. We're going to be relying heavily on these channels from here onwards.*

Part 4 – Adding Depth

Now that we have our basic shapes, we're ready to start adding color, depth, and texture.

1 Adding color and shadow

Open the Layers palette, click on [icon] and select Layer > New > Background From Layer.

Select the 'Interface' layer, and check the [icon] box to lock its transparency.

Use the Color palette to set the foreground color to R:130, G:175, B:180 and press ALT/OPT+BACKSPACE to fill the selection with this color.

Now click on [icon] and select Drop Shadow. In the Layer Styles dialog, change Opacity to 50% and hit OK.

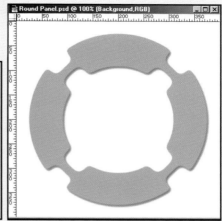

2 Adding the insets

With the 'Interface' layer still selected, press CTRL/CMD+ALT/OPT+6 and hit DELETE.

Now ALT/OPT-click on [icon] to create a new layer called "Insets". Use the Color palette to set the foreground color to R:75, G:15, B:180 and press ALT/OPT+BACKSPACE to fill the selected area. Hit CTRL/CMD+D to drop the selection.

Now we have our interface shape on one layer and our buttons on another, we're ready to add some depth.

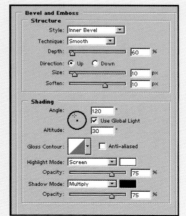

3 Giving the insets depth

Click on [icon] and select Bevel and Emboss. In the Layer Styles dialog, change Depth to 60%, Size to 10 pixels, and Soften to 10 pixels. Hit OK to confirm.

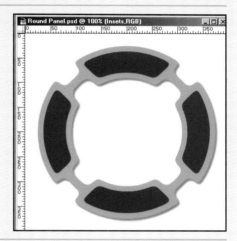

Part 5 – Adding Texture

One of the great things about working with Layer Styles is that we can easily add a texture to the interface without affecting the shading. You can add your own texture or use the following instructions to create one from scratch.

1 Creating a texture

Click on [icon] to create a new layer. Press D to set default colors, and press CTRL/CMD+BACKSPACE to fill the new layer with white.

Now apply Filter > Noise > Add Noise (with Amount set to 100%, Gaussian distribution, and Monochromatic checked), followed by Filter > Blur > Gaussian Blur (with a Radius of 2).

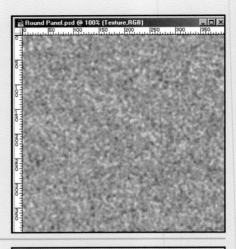

2 Fine-tuning the texture

Apply Filter > Sketch > Chrome with Detail set to 8 and Smoothness set to 10.

Press CTRL/CMD+L to open the Levels dialog and set Input Levels to 85, 1.00, and 205. Hit OK.

Finally, hit CTRL/CMD+U to open the Hue/Saturation dialog. Turn on the Colorize option, set Hue to 180, Saturation to 25, and Lightness to −20, and hit OK to apply.

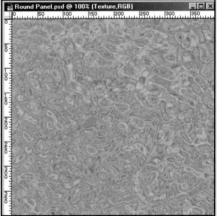

3 Applying the texture

Select Edit > Define Pattern and name the pattern "border pattern".

Now delete the temporary texture layer by dragging it onto the [trash] button.

Activate the 'Interface' layer (which should have its Transparency lock [icon] still checked) and select Edit > Fill. Specify the 'border pattern' pattern that we just created, and hit OK.

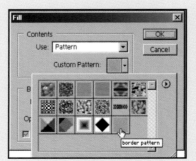

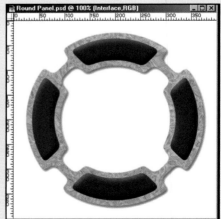

Part 6 – Grooves and Added Touches

Having an interesting shape for an interface is usually not enough. Just a few added touches can often make a great deal of difference, making an ok-looking design truly great. Let's add some extra touches to the interface to make it just a bit more interesting.

1 Setting up

Open the Swatches palette and ALT/OPT-click on 'Pure Violet' to set the background color. Now activate the 'Background' layer and select Filter > Render > Clouds.

ALT/OPT-drag the 'Interface' layer onto 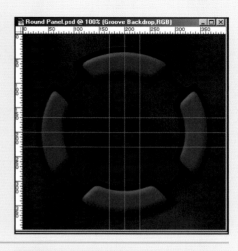 to create a duplicate layer called "Groove Backdrop". Drag the duplicate's layer effects onto the 🗑 button and press ALT/OPT+BACKSPACE to fill the layer with black.

Press CTRL/CMD+H to show the guides we placed earlier, and add vertical and horizontal guides at 170 and 230 pixels.

2 Making a selection

Drag the window out a little (so that you have a small border around the image) and press L, SHIFT+L to select the Polygonal Lasso tool 🔗.

Click first on the cross-section of guides at 200 pixels across, 200 pixels down. Next, click at the intersection of the vertical guide at 170 pixels across and the top of the stage. To complete the selection, double-click at 230 pixels across the top.

Now hold down the SHIFT key while you make similar selections on each of the other sides.

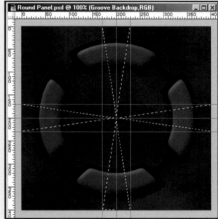

3 Blending in

Press V and hit SHIFT+CTRL/CMD+I to invert the selection. Now press DELETE.

Press SHIFT+ALT/OPT+O, 5 (to change the blend mode to Overlay with 50% opacity).

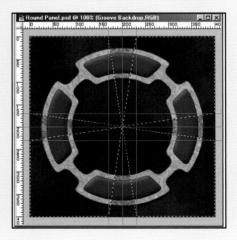

4 Adding shadows

Create a new layer called "Groove Shadows" and select Edit > Stroke. Change the Width to 1 pixel and change the color to Black. Location should be Center and the rest of the defaults are fine. Hit OK to apply.

Now hit Ctrl/Cmd+D to deselect and U, Shift+U to select the Line tool. In the Options bar, set Weight to 1px. Use the guides to help you draw one vertical line and one horizontal line across the middle of the image. Press Ctrl/Cmd+E to merge them down to the 'Groove Shadows' layer and Ctrl/Cmd+H to hide the guides when you've finished.

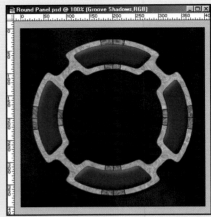

5 Adding highlights

Alt/Opt-drag the 'Groove Shadows' layer onto 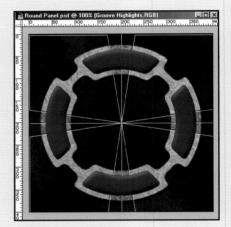 and name the duplicate 'Groove Highlights'. Hit V to select the Move tool and press the right arrow key to nudge the contents of the layer over by one pixel. Now hit the down arrow key twice to nudge down by two pixels.

Turn on the transparency lock for the 'Groove Highlights' layer and press D, Ctrl/Cmd+Backspace to fill the layer with white.

6 Trimming down

Ctrl/Cmd-click on the 'Interface' layer to load its transparency mask as a selection, and hit Shift+Ctrl/Cmd+I to invert the area of that selection. Make sure the 'Groove Highlights' layer is still active and press Delete. Now activate the 'Groove Shadows' layer and press Delete again. Press Ctrl/Cmd+D to drop the selection.

Change the opacity of the 'Groove Highlights' layer to 30%, and change that of the 'Groove Shadows' layer to 50%.

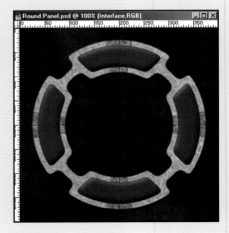

The Finished Product

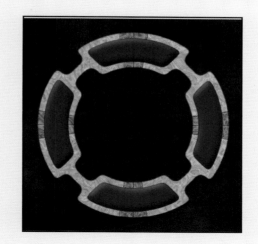

Variations and Applications

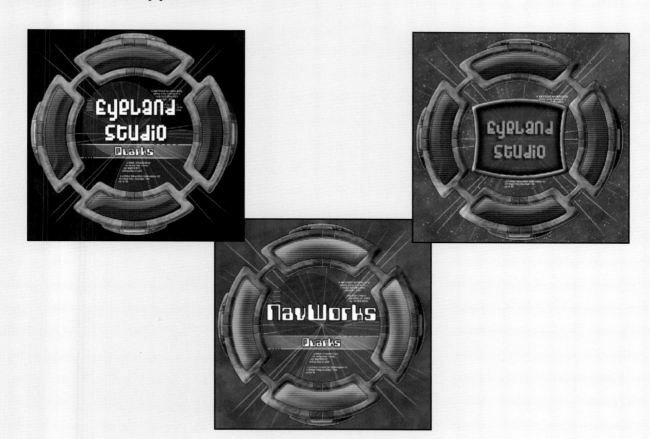

Advanced Interface Templates

Part 1 – S-Curve

A very popular shape for interface design is the S-Curve shape, and with just a little preparation, this shape can be very easy to create. This effect also uses some Photoshop features we haven't used much in this book: the Rounded Rectangle tool and paths. If paths intimidate you, don't worry. We can easily get paths to do our bidding with a few well-placed guides.

1 A new document

Create a new document, sized 600 x 200 pixels, with a transparent background. If necessary, press CTRL/CMD+R to show the rulers. Place horizontal guides at 50, 100, and 150 pixels and vertical guides at 25 and 575 pixels. Press D to set default colors.

Now select the Rounded Rectangle tool on the Options bar, and click the button. Change Radius to 50 pixels and make sure anti-aliasing is turned on.

Draw a rectangle from the intersection of the vertical guide at 25 pixels and the horizontal guide at 50 pixels to the intersection of the vertical guide at 575 pixels and the horizontal guide at 150 pixels.

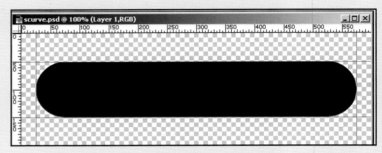

By setting Radius to 50 pixels, we ensure that the rounded rectangle will have circular endings. Because the Radius value sets the radius for each corner of the rounded rectangle, our 100-pixel tall rectangle will be nicely rounded.

2 Setting guides

Place six more guides: vertical guides at 150, 225, 300, and 375 pixels, and horizontal guides at 100 and 175 pixels.

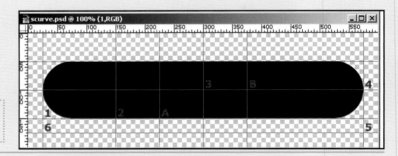

For easy reference, I have labeled the important guide intersections as shown in the figure.

3 Drawing a bezier curve

Select the Pen tool and make sure that View > Snap is enabled. Create a bezier path by using the labeled guide intersections: click on point 1; then click on point 2, *drag* to point A, and release; click on point 3, drag to point B, and release; click on each of points 4, 5, and 6, and close the path by clicking on point 1.

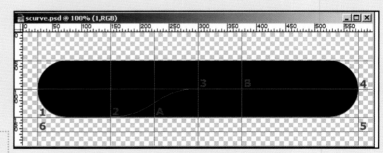

The completed path consists of sharp corners except for the S-shaped curve between points 2 and 3.

4 Convert to selection

Right-click (CTRL-click on a Mac) on the image and select Make Selection from the pop-up menu. Leave the default settings in the Make Selection dialog and click OK.

Press DELETE to clear the area we defined with the bezier path, and press CTRL/CMD+D to drop the selection.

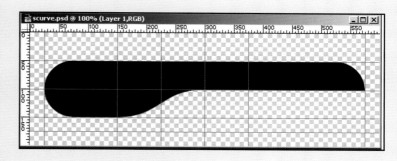

> *The result looks a little strange on the far right side, so let's work on making it rounded.*

5 Deleting the sharp end

Use the Rectangular Marquee tool [⬚] to make a selection around the right end of the shape, including the curved region.

Press DELETE and then CTRL/CMD+D to drop the selection.

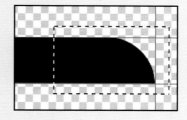

6 Adding a rounded end

Once again, select the Rounded Rectangle tool [◯]. With the aid of the guides in the upper right portion of the canvas, create a new, curved right end of the shape, as shown in the figure.

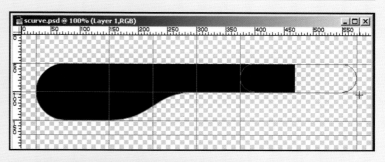

The guides are no longer needed, so you can hide them by pressing CTRL/CMD+H. Press D to set default colors, and ALT/OPT+BACKSPACE to fill the selection with black.

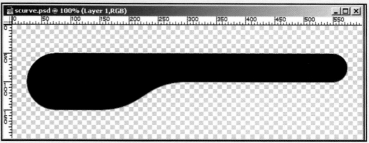

> *As you can see, it's easy to create precise shapes by combining shape primitives and bezier paths. Guides can make the task of aligning shapes a no-brainer.*

Part 2 – Complex Borders

Interfaces often benefit from emphasized borders and dimensional bevel effects. This sort of thing works particularly well for display screens and buttons, but can be equally effective just to add interesting contours to an existing object. In this example, we'll add a thick border around our S-Curve shape.

1 Creating the border

Begin by renaming the top layer "basic shape". Hold down ALT/OPT, and drag the 'basic shape' layer onto the ▣ button in the Layers palette. Rename the duplicate layer "border" and click OK. Hide the 'basic shape' layer by clicking its 👁 icon in the Layers palette.

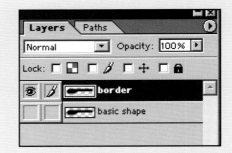

2 Contracting the border

CTRL/CMD-click on the 'basic shape' layer to load its transparency mask as a selection. Open the Select > Modify > Contract dialog, type a value of 10 pixels, and click OK. Press DELETE and press CTRL/CMD+D to drop the selection.

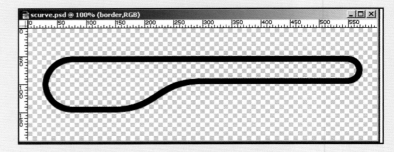

3 Adding a curved support

Let's add a curved support piece to the shape to make it a more interesting framework. Once again, hold down ALT/OPT and drag the 'basic shape' layer onto the ▣ button. Name this copy "support" and click OK. Press CTRL/CMD+I to invert the layer, making it contrast with the 'border' layer. Open the Filter > Other > Maximum dialog, select a Radius of 5 pixels, and click OK. Although it isn't visually evident, the Maximum filter has contracted the 'support' shape.

We contract the 'support' shape in order to keep the shape edges separate – otherwise, jagged edges may appear when the shapes are overlapped.

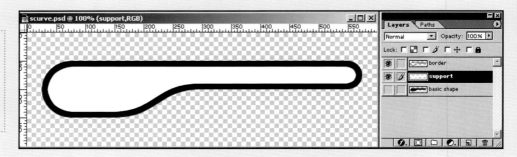

4 Making holes

Select the Elliptical Marquee tool [icon]. Hold down the SHIFT key while you drag out three circles, so as to form a single selection consisting of three separate areas. Press DELETE to erase the elliptical areas from the 'support' layer, and CTRL/CMD+D to drop the selection.

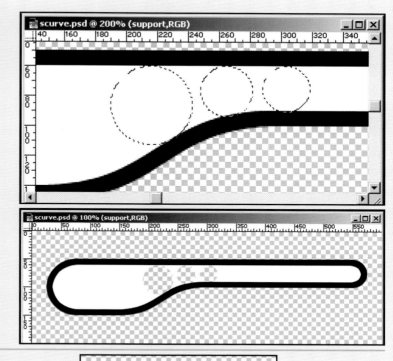

5 Removing white pixels

Use the Lasso tool [icon] to draw a selection that encompasses all the white pixels to the left of the leftmost hole (as shown in the figure) and press DELETE to erase the area.

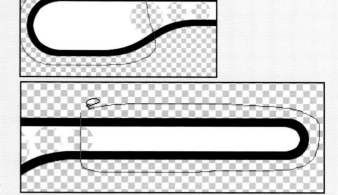

Now select the white area to the right of the rightmost circular hole, and press DELETE.

6 Matching supports

Press CTRL/CMD+D to drop the selection and CTRL/CMD+I to invert the color of the supports, so that they match the rest of the frame.

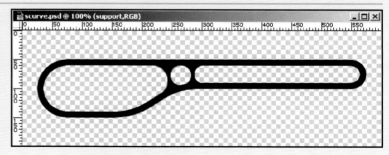

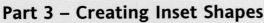

Part 3 – Creating Inset Shapes

Another simple and effective interface shape technique involves re-shaping objects such that one appears to fit inside another. Consider a capsule shape, in which one hemisphere is tucked inside another, slightly larger hemisphere. To demonstrate a couple of examples, let's continue from the previous example and add to our interface.

1 Creating the 'banner' layer

Add a new vertical guide at 270 pixels. Click on the 'support' layer in the Layers palette to activate it. ALT/OPT-click the ⬛ button on the Layers palette to create a new layer named "banner".

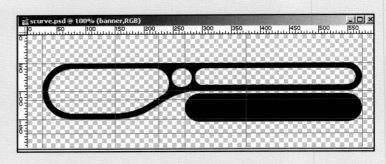

Now press D and select the Rounded Rectangle tool ⬛. Create a rounded rectangle shape as shown in the figure by dragging the mouse cursor from the guides at (270, 100) down to the guides at (575, 150). Then, hold down SHIFT+CTRL/CMD and press the down arrow key five times, nudging the shape to just below the main framework piece.

2 Making a shell for the banner

ALT/OPT-drag the 'banner' layer onto the ⬛ button to create a new layer named "banner shell". Select Image > Adjust > Brightness/Contrast, crank the Brightness up as high as it will go, and click OK.

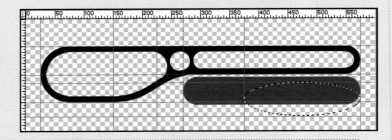

Select the Elliptical Marquee tool ⬛ and create a selection like the one shown.

> *Create some contrast between the 'banner' and the 'banner shell' layers to make them easier to see while working.*

3 Making notches

Press DELETE to erase the portion of the banner shell within the current selection, and then press CTRL/CMD+D to drop that selection.

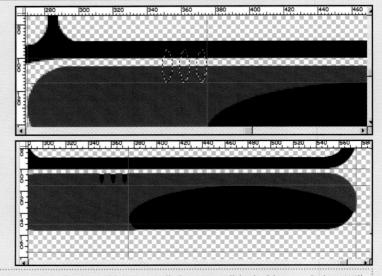

Add some small elliptical notches in the top of the shell shape by using the marquee tools to create further selections and deleting those regions from the layer.

Now apply Filter > Other > Minimum with a Radius of 1 pixel.

> *Expand the shell shape to make it look like it is encompassing the 'banner' layer shape.*

> *All that's needed to complete the 'shell' appearance is lighting and shadowing, which can easily be accomplished with Layer Styles. We'll look at a couple of finished examples at the end of the chapter.*

Part 4 – Using Shapes to Make Contours

Another simple technique for making interesting interface shapes involves copying a shape and then using its own outline to create contour lines. Keep reading and all will become clear...

1 Creating the 'button bar' layer

The guides are no longer needed, so press CTRL/CMD+' to hide them.

ALT/OPT-drag the 'banner' layer onto to create a layer copy named "button bar".

Press V and slowly drag this layer away from the original until they just overlap. CTRL/CMD-click on the 'banner' layer (to load its contents as a selection) and press DELETE. Then press CTRL/CMD+D to drop the selection.

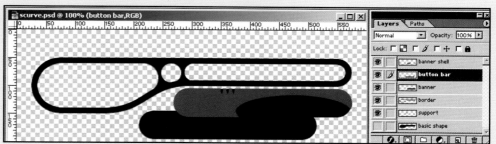

2 Contracting the button bar

Apply Filter > Other > Maximum with a Radius of 5 pixels to contract the shape.

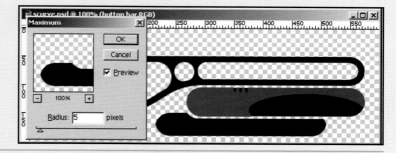

3 Whiting out the button area

On the Layers palette, ALT/OPT-click the button to create a layer named "button area".

Once again, CTRL/CMD-click on the 'banner' layer to load it as a selection. Move the selection so that it partially overlaps the button bar and SHIFT+CTRL/CMD+ALT/OPT-click the 'button bar' layer to intersect its shape with the current selection.

Select Edit > Fill, and choose to fill the area with white. Hit OK, and then press CTRL/CMD+D to drop the selection.

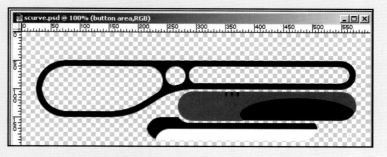

The contoured shape of the button area is quick to create, thanks to the curved shapes elsewhere in the image.

Now that you have a few interesting shapes in place, which are all on their own layers, you can begin to add color, texture, and details. Instead of explicitly explaining ways of adding colors, highlights, and dimension to the interface, you may want to look through other parts of this book for ideas on how Layer Styles can be used to convert flat shapes to photo-realistic objects.

The Finished Product

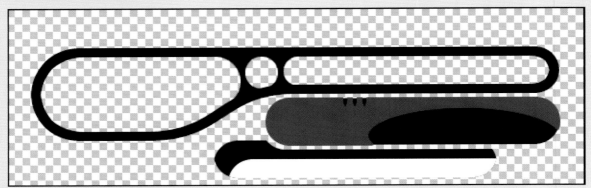

Variations and Applications

SECTION 9: BUTTONS

Photoshop comes with a number of Layer Style presets that make it very easy to create simple interface buttons with a fairly crude three-dimensional look to them. Getting your buttons to look realistic takes a little more effort though, and as you'll see, there are a few subtle tricks we can use to make 3D button effects that look just right.

9.1 Rectangular Button

9.2 Round Button

9.3 Advanced Round Button

9.4 Advanced Pill Button

Rectangular Button

Let's start by looking at how to make a simple 3D beveled button.

1 Creating the rectangle

Start by clicking on the Swatches palette to set the Foreground color to 'Pure Yellow Orange'. Next, ALT/OPT-click on '50% Gray' to set the Background color.

Press CTRL/CMD+N to create a new RGB document, 310 pixels wide by 80 pixels high at 72 pixels/inch, with Contents set to Background Color. Press SHIFT+CTRL/CMD+S to save the file as rectangular_button.psd.

ALT/OPT-click on 🖺 to create a new layer called "Bevel Button", and press ALT/OPT+BACKSPACE to fill it with orange. Now click on ◲ in the Layers palette to lock the layer's transparency.

Select Image > Canvas Resize, set Width to 350, Height to 120, and hit OK.

2 Adding depth to the rectangle

Click on the 🔘 button and select Bevel and Emboss.

Under the Structure settings change Technique to Chisel Hard, Depth to 1000%, and Size to 14px. For Shading, set Angle to 140°, Altitude to 25°, Highlight Mode to Color Dodge (with the color set to White and Opacity at 40%) and Shadow Mode to Multiply (with Color set to Black and Opacity at 33%).

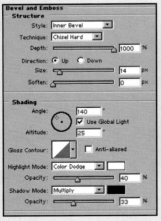

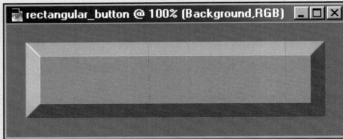

3 Adding outline

In the list on the left of the Layer Style dialog, click on the Stroke button. In the right-hand pane, change Size to 1px, Position to Center, Opacity to 50%, and Fill Color to Black.

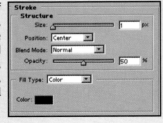

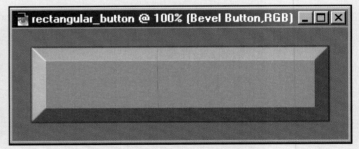

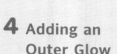

4 Adding an Outer Glow

Now click on the Outer Glow button, change Opacity to 50%, and change Size to 13px.

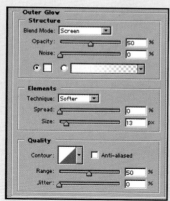

5 Putting in a shadow

Click on the Drop Shadow button, and change the Opacity to 100%. Uncheck the Global Light option, and then set Angle to -45°, Distance to 7px, and Size to 10px.

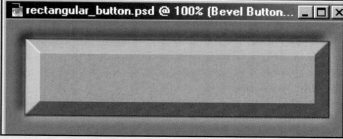

6 Writing on the button

Click on 'Dark Red Orange' in the Swatches palette to set the foreground color. Press T to select the Type tool, and add some text (Arial, 72pt) to the button. Click on the ✓ button to fix the text, hit V to select the Move tool, and drag the text into the center of the button.

Click on the 🔘 button, select Drop Shadow, set Opacity to 20% and Distance to 2px, and hit OK.

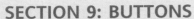
The Finished Product

Variations

We now have a simple beveled button that appears to be set within a hole in a flat gray surface. Layer Styles make it very easy for us to customize this button — if we want to change the color, the amount of shading, or even the width of the bevels, we just need to modify the Layer Style settings.

You can add a Color Overlay effect (Color: white, Opacity: 80%) and an Inner Glow effect (Blend Mode: Multiply, Opacity: 50%, Color: black, Size: 15px) to make the button appear as if it has been pressed down.

On the other hand, if you remove the Outer Glow effect (by dragging it onto the 🗑 button) and tweak the Drop Shadow effect (set the Angle to 140°), the button will appear to stand proud of the background.

You can also change the look of the button by placing different textures on the 'Bevel Button' layer. Here, I've applied a custom gradient ('Repeat White to Gray' as described in Section 11), added some monochromatic noise (Filter > Noise > Add Noise, with Amount: 10, Distribution: Gaussian), and blurred it (Filter > Blur > Motion Blur with Angle: 0° and Distance: 30px) to create a metallic look.

In this example, I filled the 'Bevel Button' layer with black, set the default colors, and applied Filter > Render > Difference Clouds several times (use CTRL/CMD+F to repeat the filter until coverage is fairly even). I then used Image > Adjust > Hue/Saturation (with Colorize checked and settings of Hue: 175, Saturation: 25, and Lightness: 0) and changed the color of the text.

Round Button – Simple Gel Effect

Layer Styles can be very useful for creating the look of gel (or glass) buttons.

1 Creating new document

Press CTRL/CMD+N to create a new RGB document, 120 pixels by 120 pixels at 72 pixels/inch, with a white background. Press SHIFT+CTRL/CMD+S to save the file as `gel_button.psd`.

Open the Navigator palette and click on the text field in the bottom left corner (showing '100%' by default). Type in '200' and press ENTER to zoom in on the image and resize the window as required.

Press CTRL/CMD+R to show the rulers. If necessary, press CTRL/CMD+K, CTRL/CMD+5 to call up the Units & Rulers page of the Preferences dialog, and set Units to pixels.

Now SHIFT-drag a guide out from the left ruler and position it at 60 pixels across. SHIFT-drag two more guides from the top ruler and position them at 10 and 60 pixels down.

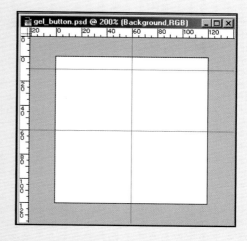

2 Drawing the circle

Click on the Swatches palette to set the foreground color to RGB Blue. Now press U to select the Shapes tool set, and press the ⬭ button in the Options bar.

Make sure that View > Snap is checked. Now click near the center of the image and hold down SHIFT+ALT/OPT while you drag the cursor towards the top left corner. Release when the circle snaps to the top guide, and then select Layer > Rasterize > Shape.

Check ⬛ in the Layers palette to preserve the layer's transparency, and hold down ALT/OPT while you double-click on its entry in the layer stack. Rename the layer "Gel" and hit OK to confirm.

Press CTRL/CMD+H to hide the guides, and CTRL/CMD+R to hide the rulers.

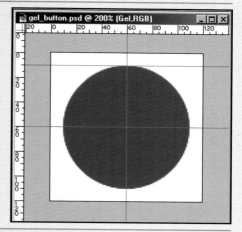

3 Adding shadows

Press the 🔵. button and select Inner Shadow from the pop-up menu. In the Layer Styles dialog, change the Blend Mode to Darken, Opacity to 50%, Distance to 25px, Choke to 5%, and Size to 30px.

Now click on the Drop Shadow list entry in the left-hand pane and change Opacity to 50%.

155

4 Blending our shape

Click on Blending Options: Default in the left-hand pane. Under Advanced Blending on the right, set Opacity to 80%, turn on 'Blend Interior Effects as Group', and turn off 'Blend Clipped Layers as Group'.

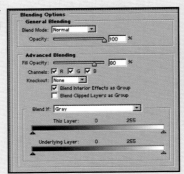

5 Giving our button shine

Press the Bevel and Emboss button, then set Size to 20 pixels and Soften to 3 pixels, uncheck the Global Light option, and set Altitude to 70°.

Now click on the Gloss Contour pop-up control and select the 'Ring' contour ◮ from the list that appears. Click on an empty space in the Layer Styles dialog to close the pop-up menu, and then click directly on the 'Ring' contour icon that is now shown as part of the dialog – this will open the Contour Editor.

Select the top right node, change Input to 96, and hit OK.

Finally, change Shadow Mode to Color Burn and set the related Opacity to 26%.

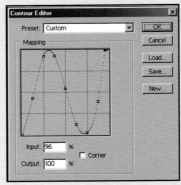

6 Finishing our style

Press the Gradient Overlay button. Change Blend Mode to Screen, Opacity to 35%, and Angle to -90°.

Next, press the Inner Glow button. Click on the color box and use the Color Picker to set the color to R: 128, G: 128 B: 128. Then change Opacity to 100%, Choke to 5%, Size to 40px, and Range to 50%.

Finally, click on the Styles bar in the top left corner of the Layer Styles dialog, and press the New Style button on the right-hand side. When you're prompted for a style name, enter "60second Gel Button", and hit OK. Press OK on the Layer Styles dialog to close it as well.

Press New Style to save the finished Layer Style as a preset for future use.

The Finished Product

Variations and Applications

Creating the entire effect from Layer Styles works well enough, but it can be very sensitive. It's certainly worth playing with the settings in the various Layer Styles, but you will find that very few settings offer good results.

It's very easy to change the color of the button – just fill the Gel layer with the new color.

In this example, I've added a Pattern Overlay effect, using Blend Mode: Luminosity, Opacity: 45%, and 'Tie Die' pattern from the default set.

The basic style works well with a variety of other shapes as well. Here, I created a new document (350px by 120px), used the Rounded Rectangle tool (U, SHIFT+U, with a radius of 50px) to create a pill-shaped button, and picked '60second Gel Button' from the Styles preset list in the Layer Style dialog. Hey presto!

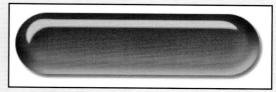

Layer Styles can even cope with irregular shapes. So long as your button layer is rasterized, you can use the Paintbrush (B) and Eraser (E) tools to add and remove regions from the basic shape – the effects of the Layer Style will adjust automatically.

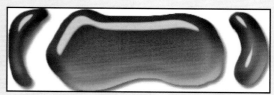

157

Round Button – Advanced Gel Effect

Layer Styles are very convenient, and once you've set them up they can save you a lot of time. However, it's not always possible to create the precise, realistic lighting effects you want using Layer Styles. To simulate the effect of multiple light sources or other forms of irregular lighting, we still need to fall back on tried and tested manual techniques – and lots of layers! Let's see another way to give our buttons depth.

1 Creating new document

Press CTRL/CMD+N to create a new RGB document, 120 pixels by 120 pixels at 72 pixels/inch, with a white background. Press SHIFT+CTRL/CMD+S to save the file as round_button.psd.

Open the Navigator palette and click on the text field in the bottom left corner (showing '100%' by default). Type in '200' and press ENTER to zoom in on the image and resize the window as required.

Press CTRL/CMD+R to show the rulers. If necessary, press CTRL/CMD+K, CTRL/CMD+5 to call up the Units & Rulers page of the Preferences dialog, and set Rulers to pixels.

Now SHIFT-drag a guide out from the left ruler and position it at 60 pixels across. SHIFT-drag two more guides from the top ruler and position them at 10 and 60 pixels down.

2 Drawing the button

Press D to set the default colors. Now press U to select the Shapes tool set, and pick ◯ from the Options bar.

Make sure that View > Snap is checked. Now click near the center of the image and hold down SHIFT+ALT/OPT while you drag the cursor towards the top left corner. Release when the circle snaps to the top guide, and then select Layer > Rasterize > Shape.

Check ▣ in the Layers palette to preserve the layer's transparency, and press X to switch the foreground and background colors.

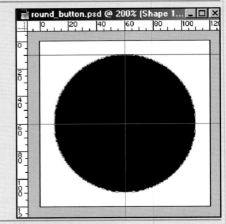

3 Adding a gradient

Now press G (followed by SHIFT+G if necessary) to select the Gradient tool. In the Options bar, select the first gradient 'Foreground to Background' from the dropdown menu and press the ▣ button so that we can create a radial gradient. Click on the center of the image and drag the cursor upwards until it snaps to the topmost guide. Now press CTRL/CMD+H to hide the guides.

Click on the ◉. button at the bottom of the Layers palette, and select Color Overlay from the pop-up menu. In the Layer Styles dialog, set Color to blue (R: 0, G: 0, B: 255) and Opacity to 35%. Hit OK to confirm.

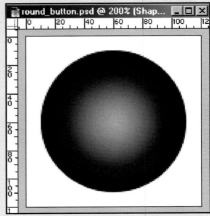

4 Creating a highlight

ALT/OPT-click on the ▣ button in the Layers palette to create a new layer called "Top Highlight". CTRL/CMD-click on the 'Shape 1' layer to make a selection based on its contents.

SHIFT-drag out a guide from the top ruler and place it at 50 pixels down. Now use the Options bar to select the "Foreground to Transparent" gradient and press the ▮ button to specify a linear gradient. Click over the topmost guide intersection and drag vertically to the next intersection down.

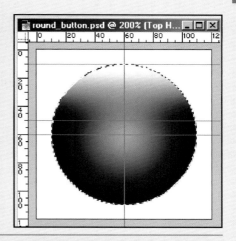

5 Contracting the selection

Apply Select > Modify > Contract with a value of 3, and press CTRL/CMD+ALT/OPT+D to feather the selection by 2 pixels.

Press SHIFT+CTRL/CMD+I to invert the area of selection and press DELETE.

Finally, press CTRL/CMD+D to drop the selection.

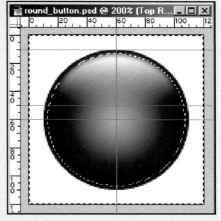

6 Further highlights

ALT/OPT-drag the 'Top Highlight' layer onto the ▣ button to create a duplicate layer called "Top Right Shadow". Press CTRL/CMD+I to invert the colors in this layer.

Select Edit > Transform > Rotate and SHIFT-drag the central Transform handle down to the center of the image. On releasing the mouse button, the Options bar should show X: 60.0px, Y: 60.0px.

Now enter a value of 45° in the ◢ field and hit ENTER twice to apply the transformation. Set the layer opacity to 80% and press CTRL/CMD+H to hide the guides again.

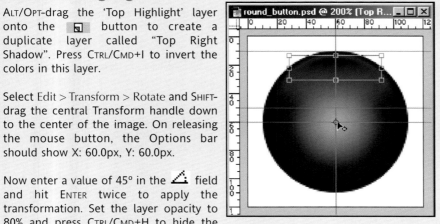

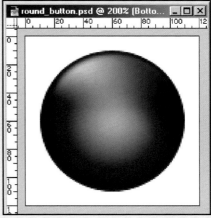

SECTION 9: BUTTONS

7 The bottom highlight

Once again, ALT/OPT-drag the 'Top Highlight' layer onto the ▣ button, and create a duplicate layer called "Bottom Highlight".

Press CTRL/CMD+T to switch into Free Transform mode. In the Options bar, set Y: 98px and ⬛ . 180°, and click ✓ to apply the transformation. Finally, change the layer opacity to 75%.

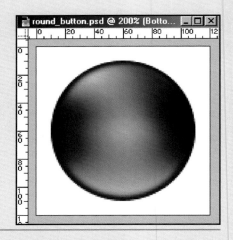

8 Airbrushing in higlight points

ALT/OPT-click on the ▣ button in the Layers palette to create a new layer called "Direct Light".

Press J to select the Airbrush tool and use the Options bar to pick the 'Soft Round 27 pixels' brush with Mode: Normal, Pressure: 50%.

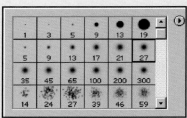

Click in the upper left corner of the button; take care not to hold down the button for too long or the highlight will become too pronounced. Now change the brush to 'Soft Round 17 pixels' and add another highlight in the lower right corner of the button.

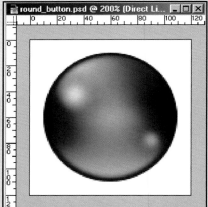

9 Adding an arrow

Click in the left ruler and SHIFT-drag a guide out to 85 pixels.

Press U to reselect the Shapes tool set, pick ⬔ from the Options bar, and set Sides to 3. Now click in the center of the image and drag out to the new guide, so that you have a white triangle pointing to the right. Press CTRL/CMD+H to hide the guides.

Right-click (CTRL-click for Macs) on the 'Shape 2' layer entry in the Layers palette, and pick Rasterize Layer from the menu that appears. Now hold down ALT/OPT and double-click on the same entry to rename the layer "arrow".

Click on ⬤. and select Drop Shadow from the pop-up menu. Set Opacity to 50% and Distance to 3px, and hit OK. Drag the Drop Shadow effect (as listed in the Layers palette) onto the 'Shape 1' layer to duplicate it.

Finally, drag the Layers palette 'Right Arrow' entry so that it lies between 'Top Highlight' and 'Bottom Highlight' in the layer stack, and set its opacity to 50%.

The Finished Product

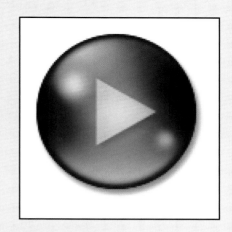

Variations and Applications

Here, I've just added a Satin layer effect to the 'Shapes 1' layer, using Contour: Ring – Double, Blend Mode: Color Burn, Opacity: 25%, and Angle: 122°.

In this case, I've added a Pattern Overlay layer style to 'Shapes 1', using the 'Clouds' pattern and Blend Mode set to Overlay.

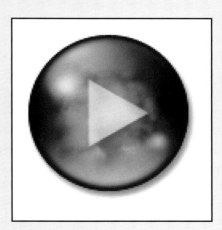

Pill Button – Advanced Gel Effect

Now let's create a variation on the Gel effect we've just seen, using the Pill shape. We'll look at several techniques for creating unique lighting effects that would be very challenging if not impossible to create with Layer Effects.

1 Drawing the pill shape

Press CTRL/CMD+N to create a new RGB document, 350 pixels by 120 pixels at 72 pixels/inch, with a white background. Press SHIFT+CTRL/CMD+S to save the file as `pill_button.psd`.

Press CTRL/CMD+R to show the rulers and Zoom (Z) into 200% if you need to. SHIFT-drag guides out from the left ruler and position them at 10 pixels and 340 pixels across. SHIFT-drag two more guides from the top ruler and position them at 10 and 110 pixels down.

Press D to set default colors, and U to select the Shapes tool set. Now press the ⬭ button in the Options bar to select the Rounded Rectangle tool, and set Radius to 50px. Use the guides to help you draw a pill shape in the center of the canvas.

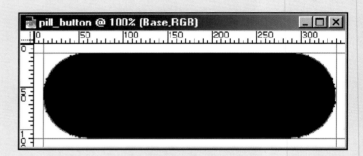

ALT/OPT-double-click on the 'Shape 1' layer and rename the layer "Base". Now right-click (CTRL-click for Macs) on this layer and pick Rasterize Layer from the menu that pops up.

Finally, check the ⬛ box at the top of the Layers palette to lock the layer's transparency.

2 Filling with a gradient

Press G (followed by SHIFT+G if necessary) to select the Gradient tool. Make sure the default gradient ▨ is selected in the Options bar, and click on the ▨ button to specify a reflected gradient.

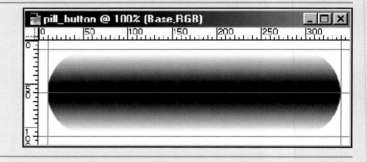

Click on the top ruler and drag a guide down to 60 pixels. Now SHIFT-drag the cursor up from this line to the horizontal guide at 10 pixels.

3 Adjusting the levels

Press CTRL/CMD+L to call up the Levels dialog. Adjust the Output Levels to 100 and 128 respectively, set the second of the Input Levels to 0.70, and hit OK.

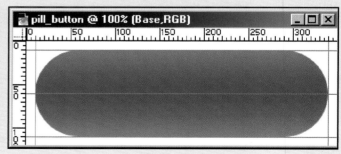

4 Adding a drop shadow

Press CTRL/CMD+' to hide the guides, and CTRL/CMD+R to hide the rulers. Now double-click on the 'Base' layer to open the Layer Styles dialog.

Click on the Drop Shadow button, and when the 'Drop Shadow' settings appear in the right-hand pane, set Opacity to 50%.

Next, click on the Inner Glow button. Change Blend Mode to Multiply, Opacity to 30%, color to black, Choke to 15%, and Size to 25px.

Finally, click on the Color Overlay button and change Color to R: 50, G: 175, B: 0, Opacity to 70%. Press OK to close the dialog.

5 Creating the highlight

Drag the 'Base' layer onto 🔲 and name the duplicate "Lower Highlight". Right-click (CTRL-click for Macs) on the new layer and select Clear Layer Style from the pop-up menu.

Press CTRL/CMD+BACKSPACE to fill the non-transparent regions of the 'Lower Highlight' layer (you'll see that its Transparency lock 🔲 is already checked) with white.

When you've done this, uncheck the 🔲 box.

Press CTRL/CMD+T to apply a Free Transform, and set Y: 85px, W: 80%, H: 32% in the Options bar. Press ENTER twice to apply the transformation.

6 Blurring the highlight

Select Filter > Blur > Gaussian Blur and apply with a Radius of 5.0.

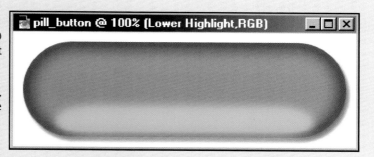

Hit V to select the Move tool, and press SHIFT+ALT/OPT+O (to set the blend mode to Overlay) followed by 5 (to set the opacity to 50%).

Finally, hold down SHIFT and press the down arrow once, so as to nudge the highlight down to the bottom of the pill.

Use a copy of the original pill to create a large highlight on the bottom half of the button.

163

7 Painting in the shading

In the Layers palette, ALT/OPT-click on 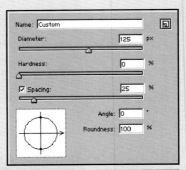 to create a new layer named "End Shading". Press D followed by X to ensure that the foreground color is set to white.

Now press J to select the Airbrush Tool, and in the Options bar, set Pressure to 10%. Click on the currently selected brush (as shown in the Options bar) to customize the brush. Set the diameter to 125px, and leave the other settings at their default values (Hardness 0%, Spacing 25%, Angle 0%, and Roundness 100%).

Move your cursor so that it's roughly in the middle of the canvas, and hold down the mouse button for about a second and a half.

Now press CTRL/CMD+A and CTRL/CMD+X to cut out this new highlight, and CTRL/CMD+V to paste it into the exact center of the image.

8 Moving end shading

Press V to select the Move tool, and hold down SHIFT+ALT/OPT while you press the right arrow once – a duplicate layer should appear slightly to the right of the original. Hold down SHIFT while you press the right arrow sixteen more times.

Activate the original 'End Shading' layer, and hold down SHIFT while you press the left arrow seventeen times.

Once you have a highlight at either end of the button, activate the 'End Shading copy' layer and press CTRL/CMD+E to merge it down into 'End Shading'.

9 Cleaning up the shape

CTRL/CMD-click on the 'Base' layer to load its contents as a selection, and press SHIFT+CTRL/CMD+I to invert the area of that selection. Make sure the 'End Shading' layer is still active, and press DELETE.

Now hit CTRL/CMD+A and select Image > Crop to get rid of any white from the end highlights that has strayed off the edge of our stage.

Finally press CTRL/CMD+D to drop the selection, and SHIFT+ALT/OPT+O to change the blend mode to Overlay.

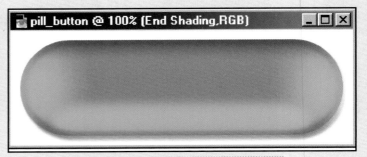

Use the Airbrush tool to add highlights to each end of the button.

10 Adding a gradient

In the Layers palette, ALT/OPT-click on the ⬛ button to create a new layer called "Top1".

Press D, X to ensure that the foreground color is set to white, and G to select the Gradient tool. Open the Gradient picker from the Options bar, and select 'Foreground to Transparent' ⬜ from the default presets.

CTRL/CMD-click on the 'Base' layer to load its contents as a selection, and press CTRL/CMD+R to show the rulers. Click at the top of the selection, drag the cursor down by about 15 pixels, and release. Press CTRL/CMD+D to drop the selection.

Finally, set the 'Top1' layer's opacity to 80% and change its blend mode to Overlay.

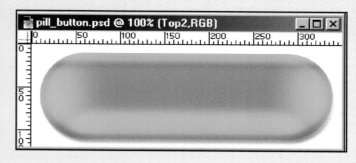

11 Finalizing the highlights

ALT/OPT-drag 'Top1' onto ⬛ to create a duplicate layer called "Top2". Press V and nudge it down 5 pixels. Then apply the Filter > Blur > Blur filter and set the layer opacity to 35%.

Create a duplicate of the 'Top2' layer called "Center Highlight" and select Edit > Transform > Rotate 180°. Use the down arrow to nudge it down five times, and follow up with five SHIFT-nudges down.

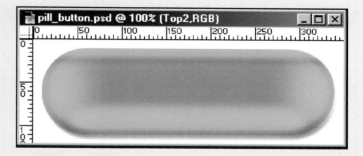

12 Adding inner shading

Make another duplicate of the 'Top2' layer called "Inner Shading", and set its opacity to 100%. Nudge the new layer down five times, and SHIFT-nudge it down twice more. Apply Filter > Blur > Gaussian Blur with a Radius of 4.0 pixels.

Make one more duplicate of the 'Top2' layer, call it "Inner Highlight", and SHIFT-nudge it down twice. Apply Filter > Blur > Gaussian Blur with a Radius of 2.0 pixels.

Now duplicate the 'Inner Highlight' layer and press CTRL/CMD+E to merge the copy back down to the original, emphasizing the effect.

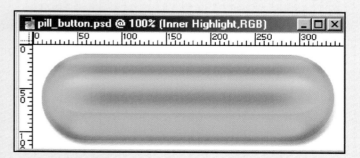

13 Adding text

Press T to select the Type tool, and use the Options bar to select Arial Black, 48pt. Type in the word "Portfolio" and click on ☑ to confirm. Right-click (CTRL-click for Macs) on the new layer's entry in the Layer palette, and click on Rasterize Layer.

Press CTRL/CMD+A and CTRL/CMD+X to cut out the text, and CTRL/CMD+V to paste it into the exact center of the image. Check ▣ in the Layers palette to turn on the transparency lock.

Now press D to set default colors and click on the Swatches palette to set the foreground color to '40% Gray'. Press G to select the Gradient tool, click on ▭ and select the 'Foreground to Background' gradient.

Press CTRL/CMD+H to show the guides, and drag the cursor directly upwards from the central guide to apply the gradient.

Finally, set the layer's blend mode to Screen and press CTRL/CMD+', CTRL/CMD+R to hide the guides and rulers.

14 Adding shadow to the text

Duplicate the 'Portfolio' layer as "Portfolio Shadow", and drag the new layer just below the original in the layer stack.

Press D and ALT/OPT+BACKSPACE to fill it with black, and set the layer's blend mode to Overlay with the opacity at 80%.

Press CTRL/CMD+T and in the Options bar, set Y to 75px and H to 75%, and hit ENTER twice to apply the transformation.

Uncheck the ▣ box on the Layers palette, and apply Filter > Blur > Gaussian Blur with a radius of 2.0 pixels.

CTRL/CMD-click on the 'Portfolio' layer to load its contents as a selection, make sure that 'Portfolio Shadow' is still active, and press DELETE to remove sections of the shadow layer that may interfere with the text.

166

15 Filling our background

Select the 'Background' layer and use Edit > Fill to fill it with the 'Wood' pattern.

Now select the 'Base' layer, and set its blend mode to Multiply at 90% opacity, so that we can see just a little of the background through our slightly translucent button.

The Finished Product

SECTION 9: BUTTONS

Variations and Applications

In this example, I've removed the background, tweaked the Color Overlay color setting, and added a Satin effect to the 'Base' layer (using Contour: Ring, Blend Mode: Color Burn, Opacity: 25%, and Angle: 122°).

In this case, I've added in the Earth texture from Section 2 as a background, and applied a Pattern Overlay layer style to 'Base' using the 'Satin' pattern (with Blend Mode set to Color Burn and 50% Opacity, and Scale set to 200%).

SECTION 10: TRIMMINGS

10.1 Segmented Pipes

10.2 Tube Connectors

10.3 Inset TV Screens

10.4 Screws

10.5 Corrosion

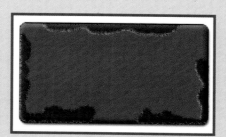

SECTION 10: TRIMMINGS

Segmented Pipes

1 Creating a canvas with guides

Press CTRL/CMD+N to create a new RGB document, 450 pixels wide by 120 pixels high at 72dpi, filled with white. Save it as `segmentedpipes.psd`.

Expand the window a little to give you space to work at the edges of the canvas, and press CTRL/CMD+R to show rulers if they are not already visible. Now click on the top ruler and SHIFT-drag down guides to 40px and 80px. Click on the left ruler and drag guides across to 50px, 200px, 300px, and 400px.

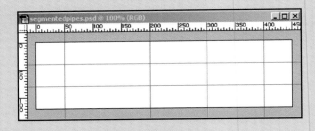

2 Making a path for the pipe

ALT/OPT-click the button on the Layers palette to create a new layer called "pipes".

Press P to select the Pen tool, and click-and-release on the intersection of the guides at (50,40) to add an anchor point. Move the cursor to the intersection of guides at (200, 80) and click and hold to add another anchor point. Now drag the cursor to the intersection at (300, 40) and release the mouse button.

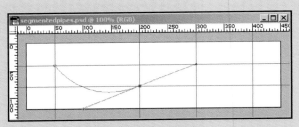

Now click-and-hold on the intersection at (400, 40), drag to (450, 80), and release.

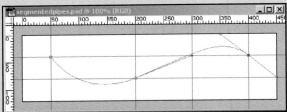

> *This path will form the basis of our pipe. Clicking creates anchor points, and dragging draws curves between these points. The direction you drag determines the shape of the curve.*

3 Stroking the path

Press CTRL/CMD+' to hide the guides, as they are no longer needed, and CTRL/CMD+R to hide the rulers. Press J to select the Airbrush tool and use the Options bar to select a 9px sized brush. Press D to reset the default colors.

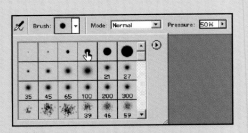

Open the Channels palette and ALT/OPT-click on the button to create a new channel called "pipe".

With this new channel still active, open the Paths palette and click on the ⊙ button to extend the Options menu. Select Stroke Path and when the dialog box appears, select Airbrush and click OK.

> *This applies the brush we chose earlier to the path we have created, so that the 'pipe' channel contains a stroke the same shape as the path.*

170

4 Smoothing the pipe

Click ⓥ again and select Delete Path to remove the path. Now apply Filter > Blur > Gaussian Blur with Radius set to 4.0.

5 Adjusting the levels

Press CTRL/CMD+L to call up the Levels dialog, and set the Input Levels to 91, 1.00, 118. Press OK to apply.

Compress the blacks, whites, and mid-tones just enough to make a sharp (but not jagged) transition along the line's edges.

6 Adding a new channel

Open the Channels palette and ALT/OPT-drag 'pipe' onto the ⬛ button to make a duplicate called "bevel". Now CTRL/CMD-click on channel 'bevel' to load it as a selection. Go to Filter > Blur > Gaussian Blur and set the Radius to 3. Invert the selection by pressing SHIFT+CTRL/CMD+I and press DELETE.

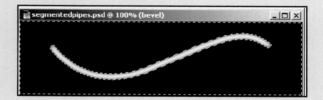

This will get rid of rough edges that the blur created.

7 Adding the 'pipe' layer

CTRL/CMD-click on the 'pipe' channel to load its contents as a selection. Switch to the Layers palette, and ALT/OPT-click on the ⬛ button to create a new layer called "pipe". Click on the Foreground Color box and use the Color Picker dialog to set R: 205, G: 41, B: 225. Hit OK to close the Color Picker, and ALT/OPT+BACKSPACE to fill the selection with color.

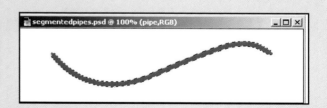

This fills the selection with the foreground color.

8 Adding the 'bevel' layer

Hold down ALT/OPT and press the ▣ button. Call the new layer "bevel". Press D to restore the default colors and ALT/OPT+BACKSPACE to fill the selection with black. Change the Blend mode to Screen.

9 Adding lighting effects

Now go to Filter > Render > Lighting Effects. Enter the settings shown opposite, and click OK.

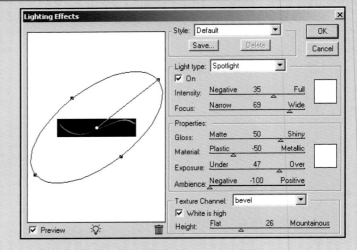

Press CTRL/CMD+D to drop the selection.

> *Selecting 'bevel' as the Texture Channel brings into effect the gaussian blur we added to the 'bevel' channel earlier.*

10 Adding some lines

Hold down ALT/OPT and click the ▣ button. Call the new layer "lines".

Hold down SHIFT and press U to cycle through the Shape tools until the Line tool is selected. Use the Options bar to set Weight to 2px, and draw some sets of black lines across the pipe as shown below. Select Layer > Rasterize > Layer to rasterize the layer.

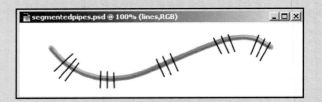

11 Modifying the line texture

CTRL/CMD-click on the 'lines' layer to load its contents as a selection. Press the up arrow key, then the left arrow key, so as to nudge the selection area slightly. Now invert the area of selection by pressing CTRL/CMD+SHIFT+I.

Press CTRL/CMD+U to open the Hue/Saturation dialog. Set Lightness to 100% and hit OK. Select the 'lines' layer and set its blend mode to Overlay. Finally, press CTRL/CMD+D to drop the selection.

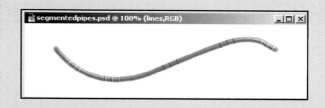

12 Adding a shadow

CMD/CTRL-click the 'pipe' layer to load its contents as a selection, and make sure the 'lines' layer is active. Now press SHIFT+CTRL/CMD+I to invert the area of the selection, DELETE to remove lines from the area outside the pipe, and CTRL/CMD+D to drop the selection.

Now activate the 'pipe' layer, click on the button in the Layers palette, and select Drop Shadow from the pop-up menu. Leave the default settings and just click OK.

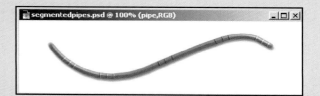

The Finished Product

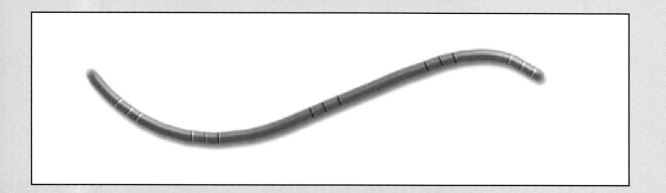

Variations and Applications

This variation uses curved lines to segment the pipe, creating more of a 3D effect. I used a black airbrush to add shadows to the pipe itself (applied using the Overlay blend mode), and added a realistic shadow to the background by blurring (Filter > Blur > Blur, *applied three times) and transforming (CTRL/CMD+T) a copy of the pipe filled with black.*

Here you can see the same technique being put to use in an industrial interface. These pipes and the illusion of 3D took several hours to make ands lots of trial and error methods. Using the right curves and shadows can make for a really nice 3D pipe!

In this case, I added another, broader pipe on top of the original. By erasing sections of the 'pipe' channel before creating any other channels or layers from it, I created natural looking gaps where the original pipe shows through. It was then just a matter of adding a 1px stroke and a background.

Here I've used dual-layered pipes to connect a TV screen with various selection buttons.

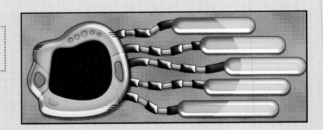

This example shows the segmented pipe in use alongside a dual-layered pipe and several other effects!

Tube Connectors

Let's make those tubes connect to something. We will make some connectors for the tubes to go into so it won't look so empty.

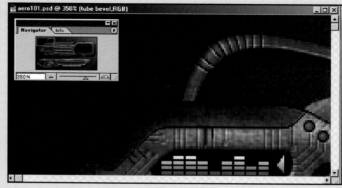

1 The interface

Open up `aero 101.psd` from the download files, and zoom in on the top left corner. Save a copy of the file as `connectors.psd`.

> This shows where a tube runs behind the interface, but doesn't actually appear to be connected to it.

2 Selecting the connector area

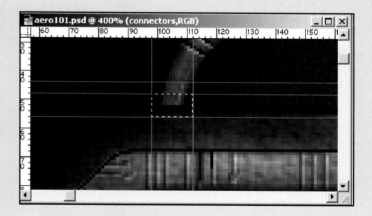

Activate the 'tube bevel' layer in the Layers palette and ALT/OPT-click the ▣ button to create a new layer (above 'tube bevel' and below 'chip pattern') called "connectors".

Click on the Foreground Color box, and enter values R:100, G:100, B:100, setting the color to a medium gray. Hold down SHIFT and click M until the Rectangular Marquee tool is selected. Press CTRL/CMD+' to show guides, and zoom in to 400%.

Now drag out a rectangular selection as in the screenshot opposite.

3 Completing the connector shape

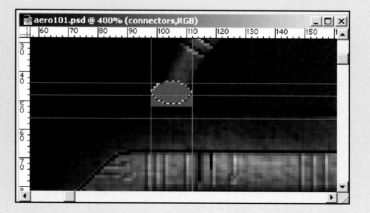

Press ALT/OPT+BACKSPACE to fill the selection with gray. Only half the box will show as filled, as the layer is partially hidden by the interface layers.

Now press SHIFT+M to select the Elliptical Marquee tool and drag out an elliptical selection as shown. Once again, press ALT/OPT+BACKSPACE to fill the selection with gray.

> This creates the basic shape of the connector.

4 Adding depth

Press CTRL/CMD+D to deselect the ellipse.

Double-click the 'connectors' layer. In the Layer Style dialog select Bevel and Emboss and click on the text to bring up the settings. Leave the default values except for Soften, which you should set to 4px.

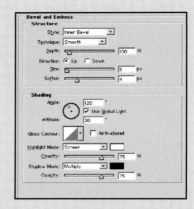

5 Finishing the connector

Select Stroke, set Color to black and Size to 1px, and click OK.

Click CTRL/CMD +H to hide the guides, Z to select the Zoom tool and ALT/OPT-click on the canvas to zoom out to 100%. Press V to select the Move tool, and using the arrow keys to nudge the position of the connector until you are happy with it.

The Finished Product

Variations and Applications

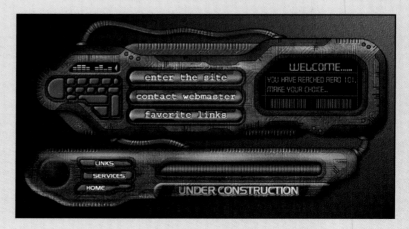

Inset TV Screens

1 Starting out with a TV base

Open up `tvbase.psd` from the download files, and save a copy as `technotv.psd`.

> *This will form the surround for our inset TV screen. I made this shape using the Pen tool, and got the depth by using the Plastic Type technique featured in Section 5.*

2 Defining an area for the inset screen

CTRL/CMD-click on the 'back' layer to load its contents as a selection, and apply Select > Modify > Contract with a value of 32. Open the Channels palette and ALT/OPT-click the ▣ button to create a new channel called "screen".

Press D to reset the Default colors, then ALT/OPT+BACKSPACE to fill the selection with white.

Press CTRL/CMD+D to deselect the area. Select Filter > Blur > Gaussian Blur and use the value 10px.

3 Contrasting the edges

Press CTRL/CMD+L to load the Levels control panel. Set the Input levels to 120, 1.00, 139.

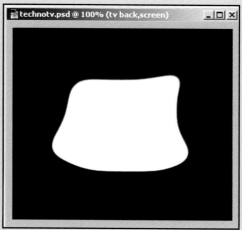

> *Moving the Input levels closer together will create a nice transition from the blurred channel to the smooth surface.*

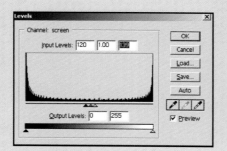

4 Filling the selection

CTRL/CMD click on the 'screen' channel to load its contents as a selection. In the Layers palette, ALT/OPT-click on the ▣ button and call the new layer "screen". Click the Foreground Color box and enter values R:48, G:48, B:48, and press ALT/OPT+BACKSPACE to fill the selection with dark gray.

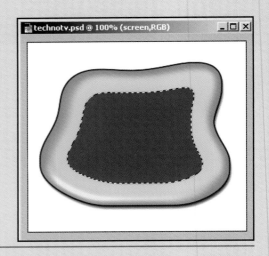

5 Indenting the screen

Double-click the 'screen' layer to load the Layer Style Effects control panel. Select Bevel and Emboss and change Style to Pillow Emboss, Size to 15px, and Soften to 16px.

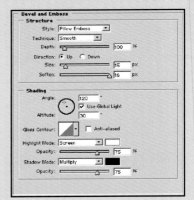

6 Giving the screen a stroked edge

Select Stroke, change Color to black and Size to 1px, and hit OK. Now press CTRL/CMD+D to drop the selection.

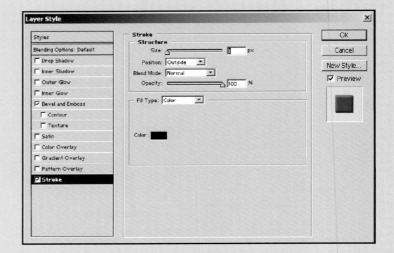

The Finished Product

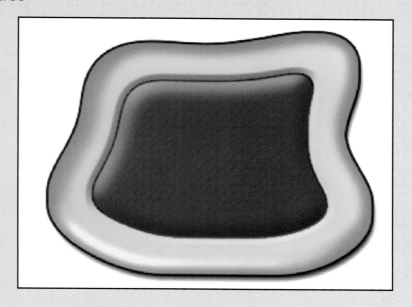

Variations and Applications

> *Here I added some pipes, indents, and some text. The indents in the TV surround were made using the same technique as the segments in the Segmented Pipe lesson. These indents need to follow the overall lighting direction used in the composite image – otherwise it won't look right.*

Cross-head Screw

1 Creating a circle

Press CTRL/CMD+N to create a new RGB document, Width: 100px, Height: 100px, 72pixels/inch, background color white. Save it as `screw.psd`.

ALT/OPT-click on the ▣ button in the Layers palette to create a new layer called "screw". Press SHIFT+M until the Elliptical Marquee tool is selected. Use the Options bar to set Style to 'Fixed Size', and Width and Height values to 64px. Click on the canvas to create a circle and position it roughly in the middle of the canvas.

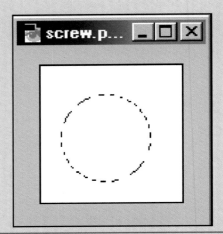

2 Adding a gradient

Set the Foreground Color to R:208, G:198, B:198 and the Background color to R:79, G:75, B:75.

Hold down SHIFT and press the G key until the Gradient tool is selected. Use the Options bar to specify a radial 'Foreground to Background' gradient, and drag from the top left to the bottom right of the image.

Now press CTRL/CMD+A to select the entire image, and CTRL/CMD+X followed by CTRL/CMD+V to cut and paste it into the exact center of the canvas.

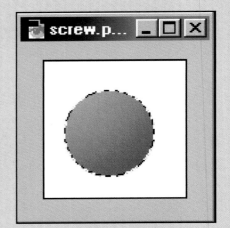

3 Adding texture

Hold down ALT/OPT and drag the 'screw' layer onto the ▣ button to duplicate the layer, and name the new layer "metal overlay". Set the blend mode to Overlay and click the checkbox next to the ▣ icon to lock the transparency.

Go to Filter > Noise > Add Noise and set the following values: Amount: 6, Distribution: Gaussian, and check Monochromatic.

This adds some texture to the screw.

4 Creating a brushed metal effect

Go to Filter > Blur > Motion Blur, and set the following values, Angle: 35°, Distance: 20px. Press SHIFT+CTRL/CMD+S, check the 'Save as a copy' box, and save as `screwbase.psd` to use in the next exercise.

> *This gives our screw a more realistic look by giving it a brushed metal effect.*

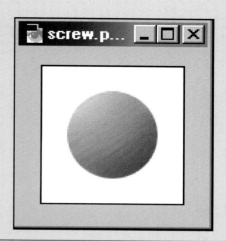

5 Creating the indent selection

ALT/OPT-click on  at the bottom of the Channels palette to create a new channel called "cross".

Now press M to reselect the Elliptical Marquee tool, set Width to 6px and Height to 44px, and click on the canvas to create a vertical ellipse. Apply Select > Transform Selection with both X and Y set (via the Options bar) to 50px. Press ALT/OPT+BACKSPACE to fill the selection with white.

6 Completing the indent channel

Now create another elliptical selection, this time 44 pixels wide and 6 pixels high. Use the same technique to center it on the canvas and fill it with white, and press CTRL/CMD+D to drop the selection. Apply Filter > Blur > Blur More to soften the edges a little.

7 The 'gray' layer

In the Layers palette, ALT/OPT-click on the ▣ button to create a new layer called "gray". Select 50% Gray from the Swatches palette and CTRL/CMD-click on the 'screw' layer to make a selection based on its contents. Now press ALT/OPT+BACKSPACE to fill the selection with gray, and set the layer's blend mode to Overlay.

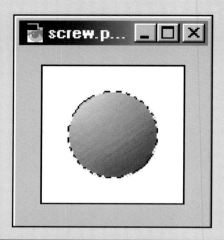

8 Adding lighting effects

Go to Filter > Render > Lighting Effects. Set the values in the Lighting Effects dialog to those shown in the screenshot. Change Texture Channel to the 'cross' channel we created earlier, and make sure that White is High is unchecked. Hit OK to apply.

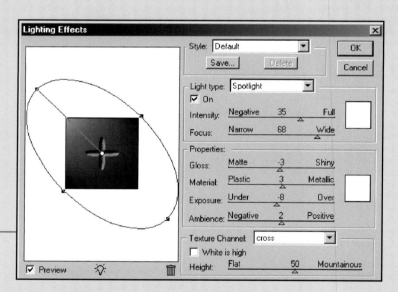

The Finished Product

Variations and Applications

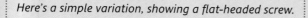

Here's a simple variation, showing a flat-headed screw.

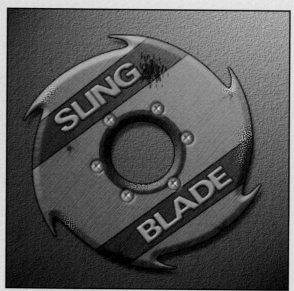

You can see the example of cross-headed screws being used in this sling blade button. Screws go well with a brushed metal, industrial type interface.

Corroded Edges

1 Starting the image

Open `rectangle.psd` from the download folder. This is a rounded rectangle I made with a brushed metal surface and some small bevels and highlights. Press SHIFT+CTRL/CMD+S to save a copy as `corroded.psd`. ALT/OPT-click on the 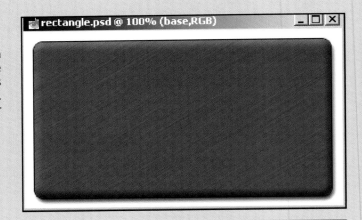 button to create a new layer called "corrosion" just above the 'base' layer.

2 Painting the corrosion

Press D to reset the default colors, and then X to reverse them so white is the foreground color.

Press SHIFT+B to select the Paintbrush tool, and pick the 'Hard Round 13 pixels' brush from the drop-down menu in the Options bar.

Draw some rough brush strokes around the edges of the image.

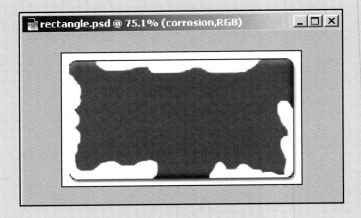

> *This will create our general pattern for the corroded edges.*

3 Getting rid of the edges

CTRL/CMD-click on the 'base' layer to load its contents as a selection, and press SHIFT+CTRL/CMD+I to invert the area of selection. Press DELETE to remove brushstrokes from outside the rectangle, and CTRL/CMD+D to deselect.

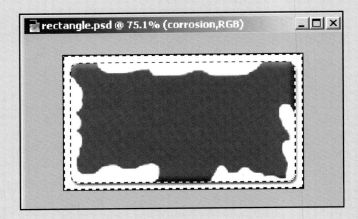

> *This gets rid of the unnecessary edges.*

4 Blending the corrosion

Go to Filter > Stylize > Diffuse. Set the Mode to Normal, and click OK. Now press CTRL/CMD+F to run the diffuse filter again. Next, set the blend mode to Soft Light.

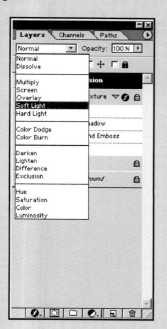

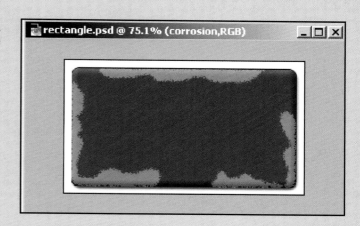

This will create a matte look over the brushed metal image.

5 Strengthening the effect

Hold down ALT/OPT and drag the 'corrosion' layer onto the ⬚ button to create a duplicate layer, called "corrosion2". Hold down CTRL/CMD and use the arrow keys to nudge the whole layer up and right one pixel. Now invert the color by pressing CTRL/CMD+I.

Drag the 'corrosion2' layer onto the ⬚ button to create another duplicate layer, called "corrosion3". Hold down CTRL/CMD and nudge it up by one pixel. Set the layer's opacity to 60% so that the effect isn't too overwhelming.

Duplicating the layer creates a stronger and darker feel for the corroded edges.

SECTION 10: TRIMMINGS

The Finished Product

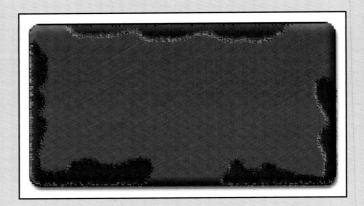

Variations and Applications

Here you can see the corroded edges taking effect on an army-style interface. As you can see, the rough edges really give it quite a different feel!

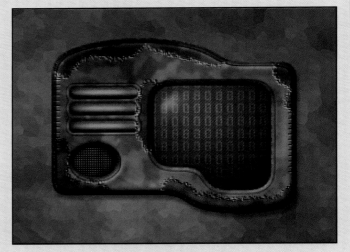

By applying the same technique to thin lines, it's just as easy to simulate the appearance of cracks on the surface finish.

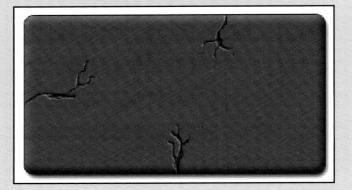

SECTION 11: ABSTRACT

11.1 Random textures (radial)

11.2 Random textures (non-radial)

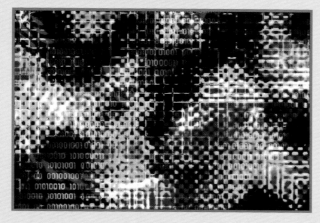

SECTION 11: ABSTRACT

Random textures (radial)

Before you start, press CTRL/CMD+N to create a new RGB image, 500 pixels by 500 pixels, with a resolution of 72 pixels/inch and a white background. Then hit SHIFT+CTRL/CMD+S and save it as `Concentric Texture.psd`. We'll use this file throughout the first half of the chapter.

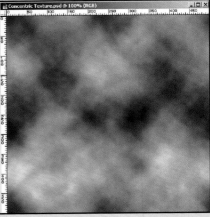

Part 1 – Concentric Grids

1 Creating clouds

Press CTRL/CMD+R to show the rulers, and CTRL/CMD+K followed by CTRL/CMD+5 to show the Rulers Preferences dialog. In the Units section, set Rulers to Pixels and hit OK.

Hit the letter D to set the default colors, and apply the Filter > Render > Difference Clouds filter.

2 Modifying the texture

Use the Filter > Pixelate > Mosaic filter with a Cell Size of 30, and hit OK to apply.

Now apply the Filter > Stylize > Find Edges filter.

Hit CTRL/CMD+L to open the Levels dialog, enter a value of 225 for the first of the Input Levels, and hit OK.

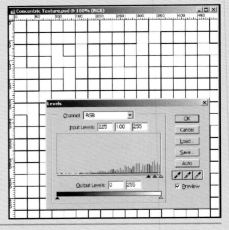

> *There are plenty of other filters you can apply instead of Levels to achieve a variation on the same effect. For example, try using* Filter > Other > Minimum *to make the lines thicker, or blur the lines and then apply Levels.*

3 Creating a concentric pattern

Apply the Filter > Distort > Polar Coordinates filter with the 'Rectangular to Polar' option selected.

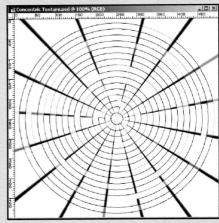

> *The Polar Coordinates filter provides the foundation for most of the effects we shall look at in the next few pages. As you can see, the 'Rectangular to Polar' setting can be very useful when you want to create concentric patterns.*

Part 2 – Stepped Gradient

1 Creating a new gradient

In the Layers palette, ALT/OPT-click on ![icon] to create a new layer called "Stepped Gradient". Press D to set the Foreground and Background colors to black and white respectively, and hit CTRL/CMD+BACKSPACE to fill the layer with white. Now press G to select the Gradient tool and click on the Gradient sample in the Options bar to open the Gradient Editor.

Double-click on the bottom left Stop marker ![icon] and use the Color Picker to specify mid-gray (Red: 128, Green: 128, Blue: 128). Do the same with the bottom right Stop marker, only set its color to white – this time you should find the Color Picker already set to the correct values. The gradient shown in the Gradient Editor should now look like this:

Now drag the bottom right Stop marker towards the left, until its Location is displayed as 10%. Now ALT/OPT-click on it, and drag a duplicate marker over to the right until its Location is displayed as 50%. Do the same again to place another white Stop marker at Location 90%. Use the same technique to put gray Stop markers at Locations 30%, 70%, and 100%.

You should now have 4 gray Stop markers and 3 white ones, with a gray marker at each end. Enter "Repeat Gray to White" in the Name input box, and press New to add this gradient to the current library. Now hit OK to close the Gradient Editor.

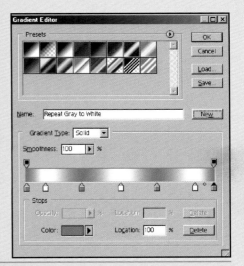

2 Adding the gradient

Click on the ![icon] button in the Options bar to specify Linear Gradient. Hold down SHIFT and draw a vertical line from top to bottom of the document. Now select Filter > Pixelate > Mosaic and apply the filter using a Cell Size of 15.

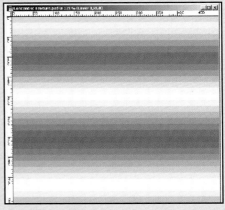

3 Making the gradient concentric

Apply Filter > Distort > Polar Coordinates with the 'Rectangular to Polar' option checked.

In the Layers palette, set the Multiply blend mode on the 'Stepped Gradient' layer, and you will see an early example of what we are working towards.

> *Individually, our effects are not necessarily very visually compelling – it's when we start combining them that things begin to get interesting.*

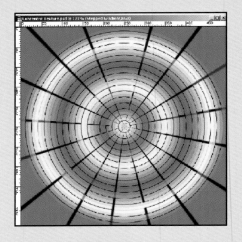

4 Adding another layer

In the Layers palette, ALT/OPT-click on 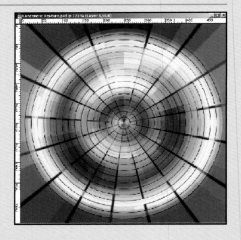 to create a new layer called "Burgundy Radial". Press D to set the Foreground and Background colors to black and white respectively, and select Filter > Render > Clouds.

Now apply the Filter > Pixelate > Mosaic filter with Cell Size set to 20, and Filter > Distort > Polar Coordinates with the 'Rectangular to Polar' option selected.

Press CTRL/CMD+U to open the Hue/Saturation dialog. Check the Colorize option and set Hue to 0, Saturation to 25, and Lightness to 0. Hit OK.

Finally, use the Layers palette to set this layer's blend mode to Hard Light.

Part 3 – Radial Backdrop Texture

1 Using the Halftone Pattern filter

ALT/OPT-click on 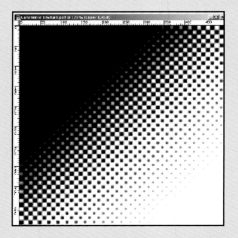 in the Layers palette to create a new layer called "Halftone Grid". Press D to set the Foreground and Background colors to black and white respectively, and press G to select the Gradient tool.

In the Options bar, pick the "Foreground to Background" gradient and click on the button to select the Linear Gradient option. Click and drag from the top left to the bottom right corner of the image, and apply the Filter > Sketch > Halftone Pattern filter with Size set to 5, Contrast to 35 and Pattern Type: Dot.

2 Creating a spiral effect

Now select Filter > Stylize > Find Edges, and use Filter > Distort > Polar Coordinates with the 'Rectangular to Polar' option selected. Press CTRL/CMD+I to invert the colors.

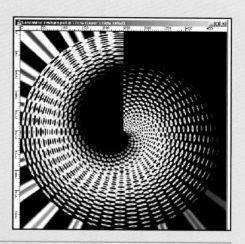

> *The Polar Coordinates filter creates a spiral effect, which can be useful, as we will see in a moment. Right now, though we are only interested in the upper right corner of the results of these last two steps. However, first we need to augment the results a bit.*

3 Modifying the spiral

Drag the 'Halftone Grid' layer onto the 🔲 button in the Layers palette to create a temporary duplicate layer.

Select Edit > Transform > Scale, set H: 80%, W: 80% on the Options bar, and hit ENTER twice to apply the transformation.

Change the blend mode to Screen.

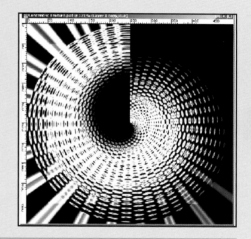

4 Getting rid of the edges

Click on the relevant 👁 buttons in the Layers palette to hide all layers except for 'halftone grid copy'.

Click inside the top ruler and SHIFT-drag a guide into position at 250 pixels down. Repeat for the left ruler, and place the guide at 250 pixels across.

Press M followed by SHIFT+M to select the Elliptical Marquee tool. Click on the intersection of the two guides, and SHIFT+ALT/OPT-drag the cursor to the outer edge of the spiral.

Press SHIFT+CTRL/CMD+I and press DELETE to get rid of everything outside the circular selection.

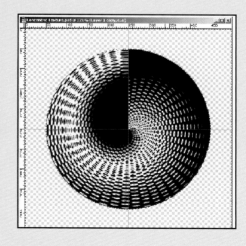

191

SECTION 11: ABSTRACT

5 Adding more spirals

Press CTRL/CMD+' to hide the guides, and CTRL/CMD+D to drop the selection.

Drag the 'halftone grid copy' layer onto the 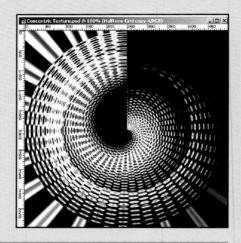 button in order to duplicate it, and press SHIFT+CTRL/CMD+T to reapply the 80% scaling transformation. Repeat this for each new layer until you're up to copy number 12, which should be very small indeed.

Select 'halftone grid copy 2' and press SHIFT+ALT/OPT+H to set the blend mode to Hard Light. Now do the same for each of the other even numbered layers.

6 Copying the corner

Now select the 'Halftone Grid' layer and make sure that all its copies are visible. All the layers in your file should still be hidden – if not, make it so. Press SHIFT+CTRL/CMD+E to merge all visible layers into the 'Halftone Grid' layer.

Press CTRL/CMD+' to show the guides again, and press SHIFT+M to activate the Rectangular Marquee tool. Use this to select the top left corner of the image. Press CTRL/CMD+C followed by CTRL/CMD+V to copy and paste the selection into a new layer.

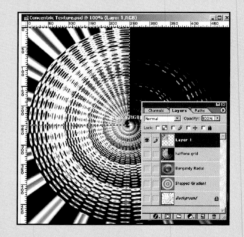

> *It often helps to make your document window a little larger than the document itself so that when you drag you can be sure to select the entire area.*

7 Modifying the spirals

With the new layer 'Layer 1' selected, apply Edit > Transform > Flip Vertical, press V to select the Move tool, and drag the copy into the lower left corner of the document. Press CTRL/CMD+E to merge the copy down into the 'Halftone Grid' layer.

Press M to select the Rectangular Marquee again, and this time select the entire left half of the image. Copy this selection (CTRL/CMD+C) from the 'Halftone Grid' layer and paste it (CTRL/CMD+V) into another new temporary layer. Apply Edit > Transform > Flip Horizontal and drag the copy onto the right-hand side of the document. Once more, press CTRL/CMD+E to merge the copy down to the 'Halftone Grid' layer.

We've finished using the guides for now, so you may like to hide them by pressing CTRL/CMD+'.

8 Blurring the copy

Drag the 'Halftone Grid' layer onto the ▣ button to make a temporary copy. Apply the Filter > Blur > Gaussian Blur filter with a radius of 5, and set the blend mode to Multiply with 75% opacity. Press CTRL/CMD+E to merge this layer down into 'Halftone Grid'.

Now create another temporary copy of the 'Halftone Grid' layer. Press CTRL/CMD+U to call up the Hue/Saturation dialog, and check the Colorize option before you set Hue to 120, Saturation to 35, Lightness to –60, and press OK to confirm. Set the blend mode to Color Burn at 55% opacity, and press CTRL/CMD+E once again to merge down into 'Halftone Grid'.

9 Modifying our effect

Now use the Layers palette to make every layer in the document visible.

ALT/OPT-drag the 'Background' layer onto the ▣ button, name the duplicate layer "radial grid", and set its blend mode to Color Burn.

Now move the 'halftone grid' layer in between the 'radial grid' and 'Background' layers, and press CTRL/CMD+E to merge it down into the 'Background' layer.

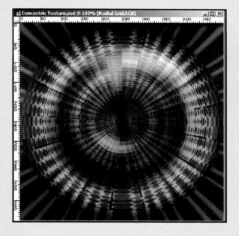

> *At this point, the layers (and their respective blend modes) should be as follows from top to bottom: Burgundy Radial (Hard Light), Stepped Gradient (Multiply), Radial Grid (Color Burn), and the new 'Background' layer (based on the contents of the halftone grid). With just four layers, things are already starting to get interesting!*

Part 4 – Random Linear Grid

One way to add some more character to a texture is to add some contrasting elements – in this case something that's not concentric.

1 Adding a grid

ALT/OPT-click ▣ to create a new layer called "Random Grid", and place it at the top of the layer stack. Press D and apply the Filter > Render > Clouds filter

Now apply Filter > Pixelate > Mosaic (with Cell Size set to 25), Filter > Stylize > Find Edges, and then Filter > Stylize > Glowing Edges (with Edge Width set to 9, Edge Brightness to 6, and Smoothness to 1).

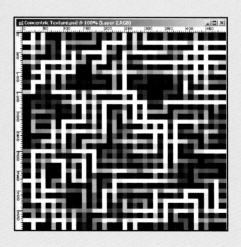

2 Randomizing the brightness

Apply the Filter > Stylize > Find Edges filter once again, and press CTRL/CMD+I to invert the colors.

Click on 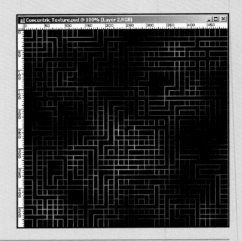 to create a new temporary layer, apply Filter > Render > Clouds and set the layer's blend mode to Multiply. Drag the layer onto 🔲 to create a duplicate, and set this duplicate's opacity to 50%. Press CTRL/CMD+E twice to merge these two temporary layers down onto 'Random Grid'.

> *We use the random distribution of the Difference Clouds filter to randomize the brightness of the grid pattern.*

3 Changing the blend mode

Set the blend mode for the 'Random Grid' layer to Color Dodge with 35% opacity.

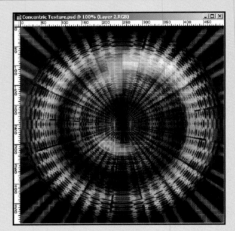

> *The texture is now a little more varied, as not all of the lines are pointing out from the center.*

Part 5 – Random Scratches

1 Adding another layer

ALT/OPT-click 🔲 to create a new layer called "Random Scratches", and make sure it's at the top of the stack. Press D and apply Filter > Render > Clouds.

Now apply Filter > Pixelate > Mosaic (with Cell Size set to 15) and Filter > Stylize > Find Edges.

Press CTRL/CMD+L to open the Levels dialog, set the first of the Input Levels to 128, and click OK to adjust the levels.

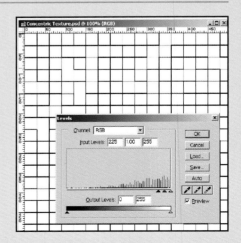

2 Modifying the layer

Next, apply the Filter > Blur > Gaussian Blur filter with a Radius of 1. Press CTRL/CMD+L again, set the first of the Input Levels to 185, and click OK to apply. Then apply Filter > Stylize > Glowing Edges with Edge Width set to 1, Edge Brightness set to 19, and Smoothness set to 15.

Press CTRL/CMD+U to open the Hue/Saturation dialog. Turn on the Colorize option, and then set Hue to 165, Saturation to 35, and Lightness to 20. Hit OK.

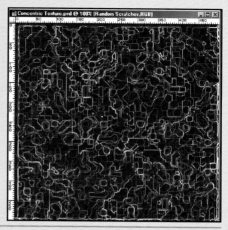

3 Changing the blend mode

Finally, change the blend mode to Color Dodge, and set the opacity to 35%.

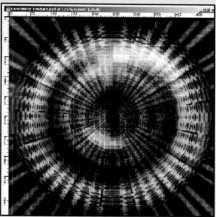

We've now added some subtle random scratches and a little color variance.

Part 6 – Warped Lighting

So far, our lighting and effects seem a little too evenly distributed. We'll now see a technique that lets us warp the lighting and distribution of the effects relative to one another.

1 Creating a gradient layer

ALT/OPT-click 🔲 to create a new layer called "Warped Lighting" at the top of the layer stack. Press D and then CTRL/CMD+BACKSPACE to fill the layer with white, and then press CTRL/CMD+' to unhide the Guides we set earlier on.

Press G to select the Gradient tool, pick the 'Repeat Gray to White' gradient that we created earlier on in the chapter, and press the 🔘 button to specify a Radial Gradient. Now click on the intersection of the guides (in the center of the document) and drag outwards to one of the corners.

Now press CTRL/CMD+' to hide the Guides, followed by CTRL/CMD+L to open the Levels dialog. Set the first of the Input Levels to 128, and click OK.

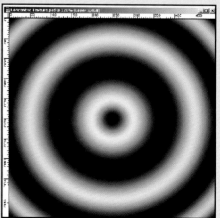

2 Blending the gradient layer

Now apply the Filter > Distort > Polar Coordinates filter (with the 'Rectangular to Polar' option checked) and hit CTRL/CMD+I to invert the colors.

Move the 'Warped Lighting' layer down in the Layers palette until it is just above the 'Background' layer. Set its blend mode to Multiply and its opacity to 50%.

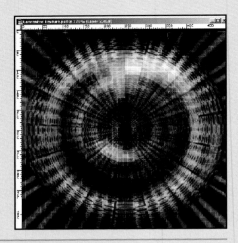

> *Notice that the lighting has become less regular, and how some of the effects from the other layers are brought out more (particularly in the top center area).*

Part 7 – Spiral Wind

Here's one more technique that will bring out some more color and add a little subtle texturing.

1 Adding the 'Spiral Wind' layer

ALT/OPT-click 🔲 to create a new layer called "Spiral Wind" at the top of the layer stack. Press D and then CTRL/CMD+BACKSPACE to fill the layer with white.

Next, apply Filter > Noise > Add Noise (with Amount 150%, Distribution: Gaussian, and Monochromatic turned on), followed by Filter > Blur > Motion Blur (with the Angle set to 45° and Distance set to 999 pixels) and Filter > Distort > Polar Coordinates (with the Rectangular to Polar option checked).

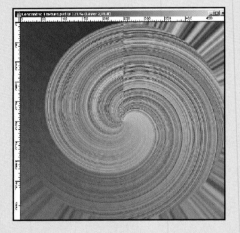

2 Modifying the 'Spiral Wind' layer

Press CTRL/CMD+L to open the Levels dialog, set the Input Levels to 100, 1.00, and 200, and hit OK to apply.

Now press CTRL/CMD+U to open the Hue/Saturation dialog, check the Colorize option, and then set Hue to 250, Saturation to 65, and Lightness to -30.

Finally, set the blend mode for the 'Spiral Wind' layer to Saturation.

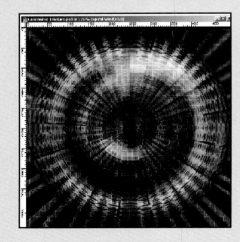

> *If you find there are more than a few streaks of gray in your results, try the last couple of steps again, but Invert the 'Spiral Wind' layer following step 1.*

The Finished Product

So with just a few creative filter mixes and blend modes we've created a rich texture from scratch.

SECTION 11: ABSTRACT

Random textures (non-radial)

Now let's look at some techniques for creating non-radial textures. We won't be relying quite as much on the Polar Coordinates filter, although we'll still use Polar Coordinates to create some non-radial highlights in the following techniques. We're going to be going for a techno/grunge/industrial look.

Once again, we're going to apply all the techniques covered in this half of the chapter to a single file. With that in mind, press CTRL/CMD+N to create a new RGB image, 700 pixels by 500 pixels, with a resolution of 72 pixels/inch and a white background. Press SHIFT+CTRL/CMD+S and save it as mosaic.psd.

Random grid texture

1 Creating the grid

Press D to set default colors and apply the Filter > Render > Clouds filter.

Next, apply Filter > Pixelate > Mosaic (with Cell Size set to 20), Filter > Stylize > Find Edges, and Filter > Stylize > Glowing Edges (with Edge Width set to 1, Edge Brightness set to 10, and Smoothness set to 3).

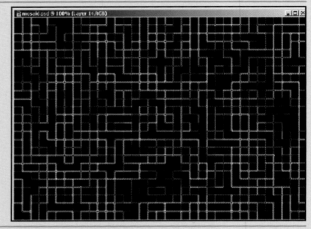

2 Adding a gradient

Click on to create a new layer, and press CTRL/CMD+BACKSPACE to fill it with white.

Press G to select the Gradient tool, and use the Options bar to specify Linear Gradient and Foreground to Background as the gradient type. Now click in the bottom right corner of the document and drag up diagonally to just beyond the center of the document.

3 Blending the grid

Change the blend mode for the temporary layer to Multiply and hit CTRL/CMD+E to merge it down to the 'Background' layer.

We have used a simple gradient with the Multiply blend mode to blacken out part of the texture. Blended textures tend to be more interesting if they are mixed together unevenly and don't cover the entire image.

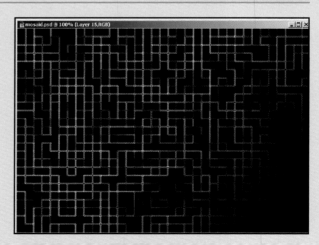

Halftone Cloud

Now we'll add a contrasting texture.

1 Creating a cloudy layer

ALT/OPT-click on ▣ to create a new layer called "Halftone Cloud", and press CTRL/CMD+BACKSPACE to fill it with white.

Apply the Filter > Render > Difference Clouds filter, and press CTRL/CMD+F to apply it three or four more times.

Now apply Filter > Blur > Gaussian Blur with a Radius of 10. Press CTRL/CMD+L to open Levels, set the last of the Input Levels to 180, and hit OK to confirm.

> *The cumulative effect of the Difference Clouds filter is to create a harsher, more textured effect.*

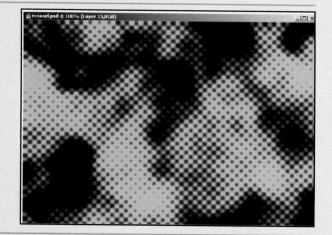

2 Changing the texture

Apply Filter > Sketch > Halftone Pattern with Size set to 5, Contrast to 15, and Pattern Type: Dot.

Hit CTRL/CMD+U to open the Hue/Saturation dialog, check Colorize, and then set Hue to 155, Saturation to 50, and Lightness to -40. Hit OK to apply.

> *Now we have a random green halftone pattern but it's a little bland. We need to add some color and contrasting texture.*

3 Adding texture and color

Click on ▣ to create a new temporary layer and apply Filter > Render > Clouds. Set the layer's blend mode to Color Dodge at 60% opacity and press CTRL/CMD+E to merge the layer down to the 'Halftone Cloud' layer.

Now set the blend mode for the 'Halftone Cloud' layer to Hard Light with 80% opacity.

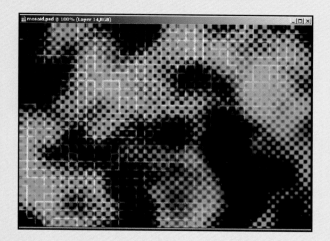

Random Tubular Outlines

Things are already starting to look a little better. The first two effects, by themselves, are not very interesting, but together they form a solid beginning for a rich background texture. Now we need some more texture.

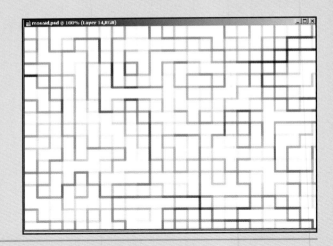

1 Creating the "Tubular Outlines' layer

Alt/Opt-click on  to create a new layer called "Tubular Outlines", and apply Filter > Render > Clouds.

Next, apply the Filter > Pixelate > Mosaic filter (with Cell Size set to 30), followed by Filter > Stylize > Find Edges.

Select the Filter > Other > Minimum filter, and apply it with a Radius of 2px.

2 Blurring and brightening

Now apply the Filter > Blur > Gaussian Blur filter (with a Radius of 3) and Filter > Stylize > Glowing Edges (with Edge Width set to 4, Edge Brightness set to 10, and Smoothness set to 15).

Once again, the distribution of this texture is a little too dense so let's tone it down.

3 Enriching the texture

Click on  to create a new temporary layer and apply Filter > Render > Clouds. Set the layer's blend mode to Overlay and press Ctrl/Cmd+E to merge it down to the 'Tubular Outlines' layer.

Now change the blend mode for 'Tubular Outlines' to Color Dodge.

The texture is getting richer, but there is a somewhat obvious shortcoming. Most of the visible lines are horizontal and vertical. We need more chaos for the grunge or techno look. What we need is a little more contrast.

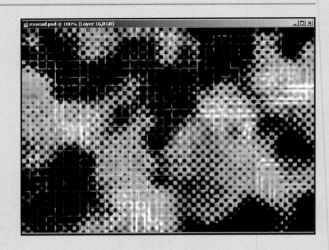

Swish Lines

Let's look at another useful technique that uses the Polar Coordinates filter.

1 Creating the 'Swish Lines' layer

ALT/OPT-click on ◙ to create a new layer called "Swish Lines", and apply Filter > Render > Clouds.

Press CTRL/CMD+R to turn on the rulers and set a horizontal guide at 25 pixels. Press M to select the Rectangular Marquee tool and use this to create a selection along the top that is 25 pixels high and 700 pixels wide.

Press D to set default colors, and hit ALT/OPT+BACKSPACE to fill with the current foreground color (black). Press CTRL/CMD+D to deselect.

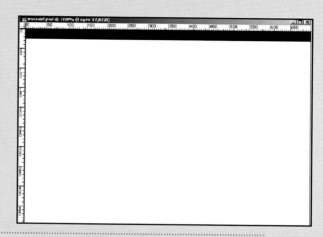

You may find it easiest to drag from the Guide towards the edge of the document. Also, making your document window larger than the document itself can make it easier to select the full width of the image.

2 Defining and using a 'Stripes' pattern

Press V to select the Move tool, and move the horizontal Guide down to 50 pixels. Use the Rectangular Marquee tool (M) – use SHIFT+M if the Elliptical marquee tool is highlighted at first – to create a new selection along the top that's 50 pixels high. This time, the exact width is not important.

With the selection still active (and the 'Swish Lines' layer still selected) select Edit > Define Pattern. Name the pattern "Stripes". Press CTRL/CMD+D to drop the selection, and remove the Guide by dragging it off the document with the Move tool.

Select Edit > Fill, specify Use: Pattern, and pick the 'Stripes' pattern from the Custom Pattern dropdown. Click OK to fill the 'Swish Lines' layer with this pattern.

3 Adding some whitespace

Position a horizontal guide at 190 pixels from the top, and another one at 440 pixels. Use the Rectangular Marquee Tool (V) to select everything above the upper guide and fill it with white (CTRL/CMD+BACKSPACE). In a similar fashion, fill everything below the lower guide with white.

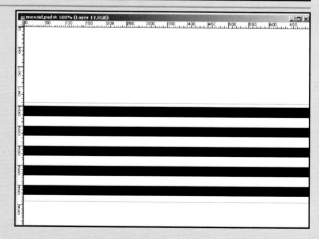

4 Adding new guides

Remove the horizontal guides and place vertical guides at 350, 400, 450, 500, 550 and 600 pixels (as shown opposite).

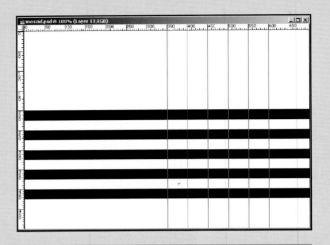

5 Stepping the stripes

Using the vertical guide at 400, draw a rectangular selection from the guide to the right edge of the document. Be careful not to select any part of any of the other black lines. Fill the selection with white. Your document should now look like the figure opposite.

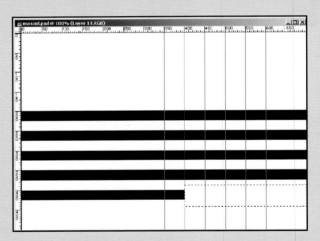

Repeat this step for the other black lines, each time using the next guide to the right to align the left end of the selection.

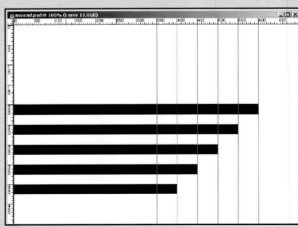

6 Flipping the stripes

Remove all the guides except for the one at 350 pixels.

Select the Rectangular Marquee tool (M) and use the remaining guide to help you select the right half of the document. Copy this selection (CTRL/CMD+C), paste it into a new layer (CTRL/CMD+V), and select Edit > Transform > Flip Horizontal. Now use the guide to reposition your selection on the left-hand side of the document.

Press CTRL/CMD+E to merge down to the 'Swish Lines' layer.

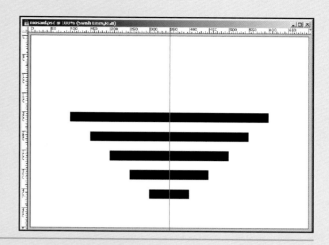

7 Rotating the stripes

Remove the remaining guide and drag the 'Swish Lines' layer onto the ⬜ button to create a temporary duplicate.

With 'Swish Lines copy' active, select Edit > Transform > Rotate, specify 45° in the Rotation field on the Options bar, and hit the ENTER key twice to apply the rotation.

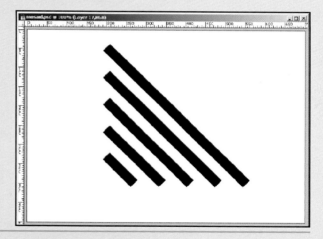

8 Distorting the stripes

Select Filter > Distort > Polar Coordinates with the 'Rectangular to Polar' option selected. Hit V on your keyboard to select the Move tool, and drag the 'Swish Lines' layer so that the lines are roughly in the center of the document (and completely covering the straight black lines from the layer below).

Press CTRL/CMD+E to merge 'Swish Lines copy' down onto the original.

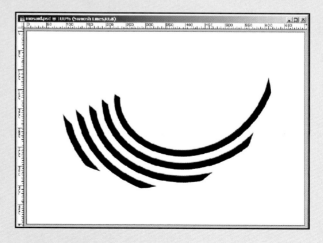

> *We now have some nice swooshy lines – but we need to do a little more work to make them fit well with our texture.*

9 Blurring and blending

Apply the Filter > Blur > Gaussian Blur filter with a Radius of 6.

Hit CTRL/CMD+I to invert the colors, and CTRL/CMD+U to open the Hue/Saturation dialog. Check Colorize and set Hue to 0, Saturation to 50, and Lightness to -30. Hit OK to confirm, and change the layer's blend mode to Screen.

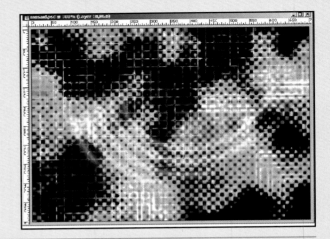

10 Adding more stripes

Now make five or six copies of the 'Swish Lines' layer. At this point, use your own imagination to resize, rotate, and skew the various copies and array them over the stage in various positions. You may want to turn off the visibility of some copies while you work on them.

For some copies, change the blend mode to Color Dodge. On others, set it to Screen and reduce the opacity to 50%.

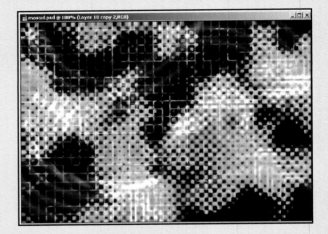

Bits and Bytes

We're getting closer, but the texture is still rather flat in some areas. Let's augment the techno feel by adding a texture made from 0's and 1's – the stuff all things digital are made of.

1 Creating some binary

Alt/Opt-click on ▣ to create a new layer called "Bits and Bytes". Press Ctrl/Cmd+Backspace to fill it with white.

Press T to select the Type tool and use the Options bar to select a nice digital-looking sans serif font.

Click on the document and type a long line of random ones, zeros and spaces – just make sure they're confined to a single line.

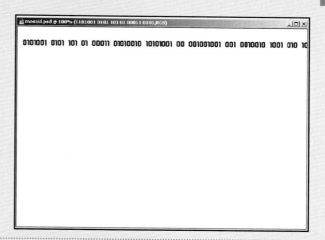

> *The figure above should give you a rough idea of the text size to use. It should be large enough for people to be able to see that there are zeros and ones, but not so large that the numbers dominate the overall texture.*

2 Modifying the binary

Make two duplicates of the Type layer and arrange them as shown. Use the Layers palette to link them together and select Layers > Distribute Links > Vertical Centers.

> *Space the lines out and move them around a little, so that there is a random distribution of zeros, ones, and spaces.*

3 Merging the type layers

Position guides around a rectangular area of characters, avoiding the characters themselves. Once you're satisfied, use Ctrl/Cmd+E to merge the various Type layers down onto the 'Bits and Bytes' layer.

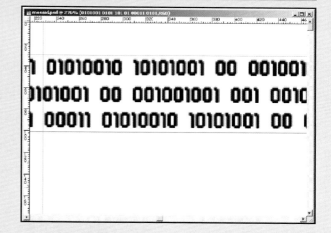

> *The figure opposite should give you an idea of how your guides should be positioned.*

SECTION 11: ABSTRACT

4 Defining and using the type pattern

Select the Rectangular Marquee Tool (M) and use the guides to help you select the rectangular area they enclose.

Now select Edit > Define Pattern to define the selection as a pattern, remove the Guides and Edit > Fill the 'Bits and Bytes' layer with the pattern you just created.

Finally, press CTRL/CMD+I to invert the layer's contents.

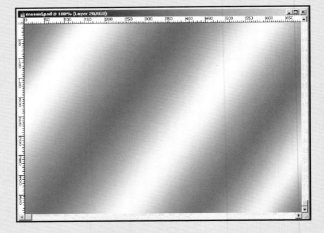

5 Adding more texture

Create a new temporary layer and fill it with white. Select the Gradient Tool (G), pick the 'Repeat Gray to White' gradient (which we created in Part 2 Step 1 of the first exercise in this chapter) and select the linear gradient option. Drag the cursor from the top left corner of the image down to the bottom right.

Hit CTRL/CMD+L to open the Levels dialog, set the first of the Input Levels to 128, and hit OK to confirm.

Press D and apply the Filter > Render > Difference Clouds filter. Then set the blend mode on the temporary layer to Multiply and press CTRL/CMD+E to merge it down to the 'Bits and Bytes' layer.

Hit CTRL/CMD+U to open Hue/Saturation, turn on Colorize, and apply with Hue set to 40, Saturation set to 35 and Lightness set to 0. Finally, set the blend mode for the 'Bits and Bytes' layer to Screen.

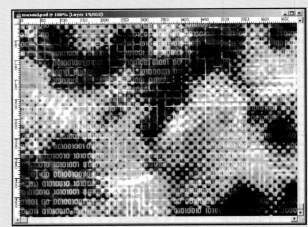

6 Modifying color and texture

Create a new layer called "Color Mix" and then apply Filter > Render > Clouds, followed by Filter > Pixelate > Mosaic (with a Cell Size of 30) and Filter > Blur > Motion Blur (with Angle set to 0 and Distance to 125).

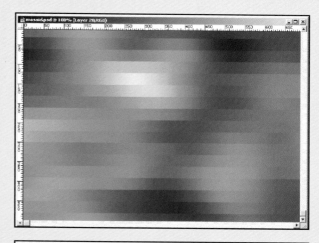

Press CTRL/CMD+U to open up the Hue/Saturation dialog. Turn on Colorize, and set Hue to 0, Saturation to 35 and Lightness to 0. Now set the blend mode for the 'Color Mix' layer to Color Burn, with 60% opacity.

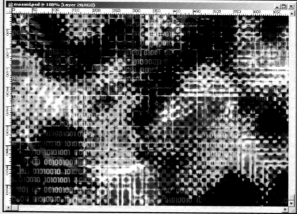

The Finished Product

As always, the supply of variations is virtually endless. Try playing around with settings for the Mosaic Filter Size, find different sources for the Polar Coordinates filter, and (of course) different blend modes with different opacities.

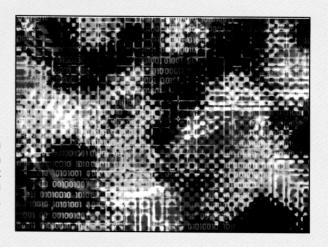

The History Palette is particularly useful for these textures. If you don't like a direction you've gone in, just go back a few steps with the History palette. As random filters are used, you may never get quite the same effect twice, so if you come across a texture you particularly like, save it before you continue working on it. Experiment and have fun!

INDEX

The index is arranged hierarchically, in alphabetical order, with symbols preceding the letter A. Many second-level entries also occur as first-level entries. This is to ensure that users will find the information they require however they choose to search for it.

INDEX